Speaking Hearts: Unlocking the Power of Parent-Child Conversations

Perry L. Davidson

Published by Perry L. Davidson, 2024.

While every precaution has been taken in the preparation of this book, the publisher assumes no responsibility for errors or omissions, or for damages resulting from the use of the information contained herein.

SPEAKING HEARTS: UNLOCKING THE POWER OF PARENT-CHILD CONVERSATIONS

First edition. September 14, 2024.

ISBN: 979-8227600646

Written by Perry L. Davidson.

Table of Contents

Dedication

To all the parents who strive to listen with their hearts and speak with their souls, this book is for you.

To the children who teach us the true meaning of love, patience, and understanding, you are our greatest teachers.

And to my own family, whose endless support and boundless love have been my guiding light, thank you for inspiring every word on these pages.

Speaking Hearts: Unlocking the Power of Parent-Child Conversations

Master the Art of Family Communication in Just a Few Months, Transforming Misunderstandings into Lifelong Bonds

"**T**he single biggest problem in communication is the illusion that it has taken place." — George Bernard Shaw.*

Welcome to a transformation journey where the art of conversation between parent and child is demystified and celebrated. This book is born from the belief that every heart speaks a language, and mastering this language within the family can unlock profound connections.

The essence of this book revolves around nurturing the threads that weave the parent-child relationship into a resilient tapestry. Here, you will find a comprehensive guide designed to equip you with skills to foster open, empathetic, and effective communication. From navigating the toddler's first words to engaging with the complex emotions of teenagers, the strategies herein adapt to meet your child's developmental needs.

I was inspired to write this book by the countless stories shared by parents experiencing disconnects with their children—conversations filled with misinterpretations and frustrations rather than understanding and closeness. These stories resonated deeply with me, echoing my experiences as a parent striving to bridge gaps in understanding with my children. Each chapter is infused with empathy, drawing on personal insights and professional methodologies to transform conversational challenges into bonding and growth opportunities.

The insights presented are supported by a blend of psychological research, real-life parental experiences, and the wisdom of seasoned communicators. I am grateful to all those who contributed their expertise and personal stories, enriching this guide's practicality and depth.

Thank you for choosing to embark on this transformative journey. By investing your time in these pages, you show a commendable commitment to strengthening one of the most precious relationships in your life. This book is for every parent or guardian eager to turn everyday conversations into stepping stones toward a harmonious and understanding family life.

By the end of this book, you should be able to navigate through sensitive discussions without fear, listen more effectively, and speak in a way that resonates with your child, regardless of their age or the complexity of the topics.

As we turn these pages together, I invite you to delve deeper into the art of communication that speaks and truly listens—where misunderstandings are transformed into lifelong bonds. Let's begin this enriching expedition towards speaking hearts.

Chapter 1: The Heartbeat of Relationships: Understanding Communication Foundations

When Silence Speaks Louder

In the quiet morning hours of a small coastal town, the fog hung low over the water like a soft blanket, muffling the usual sounds of waking life. Inside a modest kitchen, Emma stood by the window, her hands wrapped around a steaming mug of coffee. She gazed out at the muted world, lost in thought. Her son, Jamie, had left for school with words unspoken and tensions unresolved—a common theme lately.

Emma recalled their conversation last night—voices raised, harsh words that lingered in the air long after they were spoken. She remembered how his face closed off as she tried to explain her worries about his new friends. Communication had once flowed freely between them, but now it seemed every word was filtered through a barricade of teenage defiance.

Emma's mind wandered to her childhood as she sipped her coffee. Her relationship with her parents had been built on openness and trust, and she wondered where she had lost that path with Jamie. The clock ticked in the background, marking time and reminding her of its relentless passage.

The door creaked open, and her husband entered, shaking off the chill. His eyes met hers briefly before he busied himself to prepare his breakfast. They, too, had their challenges in communication—often talking around things rather than addressing them directly.

Emma set down her mug and touched the cool windowpane. The fog was beginning to lift, revealing the rugged cliffs beyond—their solidity somehow reassuring. She realized then that rebuilding trust would require more than just waiting for clear skies; it demanded stepping into the fog together.

She turned to face her husband, who noticed her contemplative stance and paused his breakfast preparations. "What's on your mind?" he asked softly.

"Jamie," she replied.

Understanding flashed across his face as he nodded slowly. "We need to try something different," he suggested gently.

"Yes," Emma agreed quietly, "we need to listen more."

The room was filled with an unspoken agreement that things needed to change—not just with their son but also between them. It was time to mend what had been frayed by silence and assumptions.

As they stood together in their kitchen—where many family discussions had unfolded—Emma felt a flicker of hope stir within her chest. Maybe today would be different; they could take a step forward together.

How can we bridge gaps when words fail us?

Can We Really Talk? The Unseen Bridge Between Hearts

EFFECTIVE COMMUNICATION is not merely a tool but the foundation of deep and enduring relationships, particularly between parents and children. This opening chapter explains why communication acts as the heartbeat of these crucial relationships. It's about more than just talking; it's about connecting on a level that fosters trust, empathy, and understanding.

Effective communication in the family setting forms the backbone of emotional security and psychological growth for children. It turns misunderstandings into opportunities for bonding and conflict into moments of learning. However, many parents face significant challenges when it comes to communicating effectively with their children. These can range from struggling to engage in age-appropriate conversations to dealing with sensitive topics that require openness and a supportive approach.

The Essential Role of Communication

THE FIRST SEGMENT OF our exploration delves into the *fundamental role of communication* in nurturing parent-child relationships. Here, we will uncover how daily interactions are not just word exchanges but pivotal moments that shape a child's emotional landscape. Every question answered, every concern addressed, and every story shared contributes significantly to building a secure attachment between parent and child.

Barriers We Must Overcome

Yet, despite its importance, communication is often where most familial conflicts begin. Recognizing **common barriers** to effective communication is crucial. These barriers can be as simple as mismatched communication styles or as complex as unresolved parental issues manifesting in conversations with the child. Identifying these hurdles early on equips parents with the knowledge to break them down systematically.

The Consequences of Silence

The impact of *communication breakdowns* must be balanced. When lines of dialogue falter or break down entirely, the effects on a child's emotional and psychological development can be profound and lasting. This chapter will discuss how such breakdowns can alter a child's perception of their safety and belonging within the family unit, potentially leading to issues well into adulthood.

This book aims to transform how families communicate by providing parents with actionable strategies tailored to different stages of a child's development. Through these pages, readers will learn the theories and practical applications that foster an open, supportive family environment. The goal is clear: ensure both parent and child feel heard and understood.

By addressing these points in this chapter, we set the groundwork for an enlightening exploration throughout the book. Each page is designed to bring you closer to mastering the art of family communication—turning everyday misunderstandings into lifelong bonds.

As we move forward, remember that this journey is not just about avoiding miscommunication or conflict; it's about creating a dialogue-rich environment where every family member thrives.

Through understanding and improving our communication practices, we pave the way for better conversations and nurturing the kind of relationships that last a lifetime.

Effective communication is the lifeblood of parent-child relationships, shaping the foundation for understanding, trust, and empathy. Through communication, parents and children connect on a deeper level, fostering a sense of security and mutual respect.

When communication flows smoothly, it serves as a bridge that strengthens the bond between parent and child, creating an environment where emotions and thoughts can be shared openly and honestly. ***Communication acts as the heartbeat of these relationships, pulsating with every exchange of words, gestures, and expressions.***

Communication plays a pivotal role in nurturing parent-child relationships and shaping children's emotional well-being.

Through effective communication, parents can provide the necessary support and guidance that children need to navigate the complexities of their emotions and experiences. Parents can create a safe space where children feel understood and valued by listening actively and responding with empathy. ***This fosters a sense of belonging and acceptance, laying the groundwork for healthy emotional development.***

Clear communication also helps set boundaries, expectations, and rules within the family unit, providing children with a framework for understanding right from wrong. When parents communicate their values and beliefs effectively, children learn essential life lessons that shape their character and moral compass.

Open dialogue allows for discussions on complex topics, such as conflict resolution, decision-making, and problem-solving, equipping children with essential skills to navigate challenges both within the family and in the outside world.

Furthermore, *communication is a tool for building resilience in children*, helping them develop coping mechanisms for adversity and setbacks. By engaging in meaningful conversations that acknowledge successes and failures, parents can instill a sense of perseverance and determination in their children. *Through open communication channels*, children learn to express their feelings constructively, seek help when needed, and cultivate a growth mindset that empowers them to overcome obstacles.

Effective communication forms the cornerstone of parent-child relationships, shaping the dynamics and interactions within the family unit. *Parents* can nurture strong connections with their children based on trust, understanding, and mutual support by fostering an environment where dialogue is encouraged, respected, and valued. *Communication is not just about exchanging words; it is about creating a profound connection that resonates at the core of every relationship.*

Continue reading to discover common barriers to effective communication within families.

EFFECTIVE COMMUNICATION within families can sometimes be challenging due to various barriers that hinder the flow of open dialogue. *One common barrier is a need for more active listening.*

In many instances, individuals may be more focused on expressing their thoughts and opinions rather than genuinely listening to what the other person is saying. This can lead to misunderstandings and a communication breakdown. *Another barrier is the presence of distractions.* In today's fast-paced world, distractions such as technology or busy schedules can impede meaningful conversations within families. When attention is divided, it becomes difficult to engage fully in communication.

Misunderstandings can also arise from differing communication styles within families. Each individual may have a unique way of expressing themselves, which can sometimes clash with others' styles, leading to confusion or conflict. *Unresolved conflicts and past resentments* can further act as barriers to effective communication. When there are underlying tensions or unresolved issues within a family, it can create a hostile environment for open and honest conversations.

Emotional barriers, such as fear of vulnerability or emotional intimacy, can also hinder family communication. Some individuals may struggle to express their true feelings out of fear of judgment or rejection, leading to a lack of emotional connection in relationships. *Cultural differences within* families can also pose challenges to effective communication. Differing cultural backgrounds influence how individuals communicate and interpret messages, potentially causing misunderstandings if not addressed openly and respectfully.

Power dynamics within families can be another significant barrier to effective communication. When one party holds more power or authority in the family dynamic, it can inhibit others from freely expressing their thoughts and feelings. This imbalance can stifle open dialogue and create a disconnect between family members.

Lastly, stress and fatigue can impact communication within families. When individuals are under high levels of anxiety or feeling fatigued, they may not have the mental or emotional capacity to engage in meaningful conversations, leading to miscommunication or emotional distance.

Recognizing these common barriers is essential in improving communication within families. By addressing these obstacles head-on and fostering an environment of understanding and empathy, families can overcome these challenges and build stronger, more harmonious relationships based on clear and open dialogue.

Effective communication breakdowns can profoundly impact children's emotional and psychological development. When parents and children struggle to connect through dialogue, it can lead to feelings of isolation, misunderstanding, and emotional distress.

Children communicate with their parents to feel heard, valued, and understood, shaping their self-worth and confidence. When this vital communication channel is disrupted or strained, it can have lasting effects on a child's mental well-being.

Misunderstandings resulting from poor communication can sow seeds of doubt in a child's mind about their place in the family dynamic. ***Children may internalize feelings of inadequacy or rejection*** when they perceive that their parents are not listening or responding to their needs effectively. This can impact their self-esteem and ability to form healthy relationships in the future.

Emotional disconnects caused by communication breakdowns can lead to a lack of trust between parents and children, hindering the development of secure attachments crucial for emotional stability.

Psychological development in children is closely tied to the quality of communication within the family unit. ***Children learn how to regulate their emotions, express their thoughts, and navigate conflicts by observing and participating in family conversations.***

When communication is fraught with misunderstandings or disputes, children may struggle to develop these essential skills, leading to challenges in managing their emotions and relationships as they grow older.

Communication breakdowns can also contribute to behavioral issues in children as they may resort to harmful coping mechanisms like withdrawal, aggression, or defiance when they feel unheard or misunderstood. *The inability to express themselves effectively* due to poor communication can manifest in behavioral problems that may further strain parent-child relationships and exacerbate emotional distress for both parties.

The impact of communication breakdowns on children's emotional and psychological development cannot be overstated.

Healthy communication is a foundation for nurturing secure attachments, fostering emotional intelligence, and promoting mental well-being. Parents play a pivotal role in creating a safe space for open dialogue where children feel supported, valued, and understood. By addressing communication barriers proactively and fostering a culture of empathy and mutual respect within the family, parents can help mitigate the adverse effects of communication breakdowns on their children's development.

Effective communication sits at the core of thriving parent-child relationships. It is the very foundation that supports understanding, trust, and emotional growth. Throughout this chapter, we've uncovered how essential open dialogue is in fostering a nurturing environment, how barriers can impede this process, and the lasting impact communication breakdowns can have on a child's development.

Communication is not just about talking; it's about connecting.

When parents and children learn to express themselves clearly and listen empathetically, they build bridges of understanding that can withstand life's challenges. The consequences of ignoring these principles are significant, leading to misinterpretations and emotional disconnects that can strain even the strongest bonds.

By mastering effective communication, parents are equipped to guide their children through emotional and psychological growth complexities. This skill set prevents potential conflicts and strengthens the relationship, creating a safe space for children to explore their feelings and thoughts.

The insights shared here are just the beginning. As you continue through this book, you'll discover practical strategies to enhance your communication skills, deepen your connection with your children, and foster an environment of mutual respect and understanding. Each chapter builds on the next, offering valuable tools and insights to transform your family dynamics.

Embrace this journey with an open heart and mind. Mastering the art of family communication has profound benefits, promising not only to resolve misunderstandings but also to forge lifelong bonds that celebrate every facet of your child's development. Let's continue to explore these transformative techniques together, ensuring that every conversation with your child counts towards building a more robust, more resilient family unit.

Chapter 2: Bridging the Generational Divide: More Than Just Good Intentions

When Good Intentions Aren't Enough

Ellen's hands, worn from years of gardening and piano lessons, trembled slightly as she lifted the porcelain teacup. The steam rose in gentle swirls, mingling with the lingering scent of jasmine from the garden outside. Her daughter, Sarah, sat across from her at the old oak table, where she had witnessed countless family meals and heart-to-heart talks. The room was steeped in silence save for the soft ticking of the grandfather clock in the corner.

Sarah fidgeted with her spoon, her brow furrowed as she considered how to bridge the chasm that seemed to have formed between her and her mother over the years. Ellen sensed her daughter's discomfort and wished she could read her mind and understand what lay behind those anxious eyes. They were both trying, stumbling through attempts at conversation that felt more like navigating a minefield than sharing thoughts.

Outside, a robin pecked at the ground beneath the window. Its movements were precise and deliberate. Ellen watched it momentarily, drawing a parallel between its search for sustenance and her search for the right words. She remembered how easy it used to be when Sarah was younger, how laughter filled their days, and how mutual understanding seemed effortless.

"Mom," Sarah finally broke the silence, "I feel like we're speaking different languages sometimes." Her voice carried a mix of frustration and longing.

Ellen set down her cup with a soft clink against the saucer. "I know, darling," she replied softly. The sound of their voices felt jarring in contrast to their inner turmoil. She pondered on all those parenting books she had read when Sarah was born, none of which seemed to have prepared her for this stage of motherhood—where intentions fell short and words failed.

The afternoon light shifted slightly as clouds gathered outside, casting shadows across the floral wallpaper that had started to fade over time. Ellen noticed a spider weaving its web in one corner—a silent witness to their struggle.

As they both reached for more words to fill the growing void between them, Ellen wondered if love could transcend generational divides or if some gaps were too wide to bridge.

Understanding requires more than just good intentions.

When Good Intentions Aren't Enough

Good intentions in family conversations are like seeds; they hold potential but require nurturing to flourish. It's a misconception that positive intentions guarantee fruitful communication between parents and children. This chapter delves into the nuanced realities that often create gaps in understanding despite the best intentions. By exploring how different communication styles, emotional expressiveness, and interests impact dialogues, we aim to bridge the generational divide that sometimes seems like a chasm.

Understanding the Communication Chasm

At first glance, love and goodwill should naturally culminate in open and effective communication within families. However, differences in generational perspectives often complicate this dynamic. The digital age has introduced new modes of interaction that are usually more familiar to younger generations than to their parents. Recognizing these disparities is the first step toward building bridges. Both parents and children must appreciate that their methods of communication may differ widely but can be reconciled through mutual effort.

Strategies for Emotional and Interest Alignment

Emotional expressiveness varies significantly across generations. Parents might have grown up in environments where emotional restraint was valued. At the same time, children today are often encouraged to express their feelings openly. This shift can lead to misunderstandings or even conflict if not navigated carefully. Similarly, disparate interests can widen the communication gap. Engaging genuinely with each other's passions can be a powerful bridge in understanding each other's worlds.

Approaching Sensitive Topics

Sensitive topics such as academic pressures or social challenges require careful handling. A direct approach may backfire, especially if tension has already developed due to unaddressed communication issues. Learning techniques to introduce these subjects gently can significantly affect how these conversations unfold.

This chapter aims to highlight these challenges and offer practical strategies for overcoming them. By fostering an environment where both parties feel heard and valued, families can transform potential conflicts into opportunities to strengthen bonds.

This chapter serves as a guide for parents striving to understand and connect with their children on a deeper level. It underscores the importance of active effort over mere good intentions. It provides tools to enhance familial relationships through improved communication.

As we explore these themes further, remember that effective communication is an art that requires patience, empathy, and, above all, practice. Mastering this art is one of the most rewarding investments you can make in your family's future.

Effective communication between parents and children can be hindered by the differences in communication styles between generations. Parents often struggle to connect with their children due to varying approaches to expressing thoughts and emotions.

While parents may value direct and assertive communication, younger generations might prefer indirect or nuanced ways of conveying their feelings. Recognizing these disparities is the first step towards bridging the gap and fostering better understanding within the family dynamic.

Understanding the nuances of generational communication styles is crucial for parents seeking to improve their relationships with their children. Older generations may prioritize respect and authority in conversations, while younger individuals might value empathy and active listening. If not addressed proactively, these differences can lead to misunderstandings and conflicts. By acknowledging and respecting each other's preferred communication styles, parents and children can create a more harmonious dialogue that promotes mutual respect and understanding.

Communication barriers can also arise from technological advancements that have significantly altered the way individuals interact with each other. The prevalence of digital communication has shaped younger generations' preferences for quick, concise messages, sometimes at the expense of more profound, meaningful conversations. Parents who grew up before smartphones and social media may struggle to adapt to these new modes of communication, further widening the generation gap.

Embracing flexibility and openness in communication can help bridge these generational divides. Parents can learn about their children's preferred communication methods through texting, social media, or face-to-face conversations. Similarly, children can show appreciation for their parents' traditional communication styles while advocating for more modern forms of interaction. Finding a middle ground that respects both parties' comfort levels is critical to fostering healthy family communication.

Parents can take proactive steps to enhance their relationships with their children by recognizing the gaps in communication styles between different generations. Through open-mindedness, adaptability, and a willingness to learn from each other, families can navigate generational differences in communication more effectively. Building bridges across these divides requires patience, empathy, and a genuine desire to connect on a deeper level with loved ones. The following sections explore strategies to overcome emotional expressiveness disparities and interest gaps, further enhancing parent-child communication dynamics.

Let's delve deeper into developing strategies to overcome emotional expressiveness disparities and interest gaps within your family conversations.

Recognizing and understanding the differences in emotional expressiveness and interests between generations is crucial for effective family communication. Parents and children often have varying levels of comfort when expressing their emotions. While some parents may be reserved when discussing feelings, their children might be more open and expressive. This contrast can lead to misunderstandings and communication breakdowns if not addressed proactively. Additionally, differences in interests can create barriers to meaningful conversations. Parents may need help to connect with their children on topics that seem irrelevant or uninteresting to them. *Acknowledging these disparities is the first step towards bridging the communication gap.*

Developing strategies to overcome these challenges requires patience, empathy, and a willingness to adapt. Encouraging open dialogue by creating a safe space for expression is essential. Parents should actively listen to their children without judgment, allowing them to freely share their thoughts and feelings. Parents can build stronger connections and foster deeper conversations by showing genuine interest in their children's passions and hobbies.

Empathy is crucial in understanding each other's perspectives and fostering mutual respect within the family dynamic.

Sharing activities or hobbies can help bridge the gap between different generations. Finding common ground through activities that parents and children enjoy can allow natural conversations to unfold. Whether it's cooking together, watching a movie, or playing a sport, these shared experiences can strengthen bonds and improve communication. *By participating in each other's interests, family members can better appreciate one another's worlds.*

Setting aside dedicated time for meaningful conversations is crucial for building strong family relationships. Regular opportunities to connect without distractions allow for focused communication and deeper engagement. Whether it's a weekly family dinner or a scheduled walk in the park, these moments provide a platform for meaningful discussions and emotional sharing. *Consistent communication fosters trust and understanding, laying the foundation for healthy relationships based on mutual respect and openness.*

Encouraging children to express themselves creatively can also enhance communication within families. Artistic outlets such as drawing, writing, or music can provide alternative ways for children to communicate their emotions and thoughts. Parents who support and encourage their children's creative expressions create space for deeper insights into their inner world. *By valuing creativity as a form of communication, parents can tap into new channels of understanding and connection with their children.*

Approaching sensitive topics with your child requires finesse and consideration. These conversations can be delicate and impact your relationship significantly. *Learning techniques to navigate these discussions gently and effectively fosters understanding and maintains trust.* One key strategy is to create a safe space where your child feels comfortable sharing their thoughts and emotions.

Active listening is vital in this process, demonstrating that you value their perspective and are genuinely interested in what they say. ***Timing is also essential when broaching sensitive subjects.*** Choose a moment when both you and your child are relaxed and free from distractions. This sets the stage for a more open and receptive dialogue. ***Approach the conversation with empathy and understanding,*** acknowledging that the topic may be challenging for both of you. ***Express your willingness to listen without judgment,*** creating an atmosphere of mutual respect.

When discussing sensitive topics, ***use "I" statements to express your feelings*** rather than placing blame or making accusations. This approach helps to prevent defensiveness and encourages a more constructive exchange of ideas. ***Focus on your emotions and experiences*** related to the issue, allowing your child to understand your perspective without feeling attacked.

Please encourage your child to share their thoughts and feelings openly by asking open-ended questions that invite more profound reflection. ***Avoid interrogating or pressuring them*** to disclose more than they are comfortable with. ***Respect their boundaries*** while gently encouraging them to express themselves authentically.

Remaining calm and composed is essential when navigating sensitive topics, even if the conversation becomes challenging or emotional. Your ability to stay level-headed can set the tone for a productive discussion and demonstrate maturity in handling complex subjects. ***Validate your child's emotions,*** even if you disagree with their perspective, showing that you acknowledge their feelings as valid and worthy of consideration.

As you engage in conversations about sensitive topics, remember that ***building trust is a gradual process that*** requires patience and consistency. By approaching these discussions with sensitivity, empathy, and respect, you can deepen your bond with your child and create a foundation of open communication for the future.

Understanding each other within a family isn't just a matter of intention; it requires deliberate and thoughtful actions. Throughout this chapter, we've explored how recognizing and bridging the communication gaps between generations is crucial for fostering a healthy dialogue. The differences in how we express emotions, engage with interests, and approach sensitive topics are not just hurdles but opportunities for deeper connection and understanding.

Goodwill is essential but not the sole ingredient for effective communication. It's vital to actively learn and apply strategies accommodating these generational distinctions. By doing so, we prevent conflicts and enrich our relationships, ensuring that every family member feels heard and valued.

The techniques discussed here are more than tools; they are pathways to empathy and resilience. By gently navigating sensitive issues, we demonstrate respect and care for our loved ones' perspectives. This strengthens bonds and builds a foundation of trust and mutual respect that will benefit family dynamics in the long run.

Remember, every conversation is a step toward mutual understanding. Your efforts today to bridge these divides will echo throughout your relationships, enhancing the present interactions and setting a tone of compassion and comprehension for future generations.

As we progress in this book, remember that these strategies are part of a more extensive journey toward mastering family communication. Each step you take is a building block in transforming misunderstandings into lifelong bonds. Embrace these challenges as opportunities to grow together, fortifying your family with every word you share.

Chapter 3: The Art of Being Present: Mastering Active Listening

Can Listening Mend a Fractured Bond?

Eleanor sat at the small oak table by the kitchen window, her fingers tracing the wood grain as she watched her son, Tommy, playing in the backyard. The sunlight dappled through the leaves of an old elm tree, casting shadows that danced across his face. She noticed his brow furrowed with concentration as he maneuvered his toy trucks through the dirt, creating little roads and pathways.

Inside, Eleanor felt a twinge of regret and hope intertwining like vines. She remembered their conversation last night—his words still echoed in her mind, revealing feelings of neglect and misunderstanding. "You never listen," he had said, his voice small but charged with emotion. It stung because she feared it was true.

The aroma of coffee filled the air as Eleanor poured herself another cup, its warmth comforting against her hands. She pondered how to approach Tommy again and honestly listen this time. Her thoughts drifted back to her childhood, recalling how her father would sit beside her after school, giving her space to share stories about her day without judgment or interruption. She cherished those moments of being heard—it was a gift she now realized she needed to give to Tommy.

As she sipped her coffee, Eleanor resolved to foster an atmosphere where open conversations could flourish. She imagined sitting with Tommy on the porch swing, encouraging him to express his thoughts and feelings while she practiced active listening—being fully present and empathetic.

A gentle breeze rustled through the kitchen curtains as Eleanor set down her cup with newfound determination. Today could be different; it needed to be different for both their sakes.

How can active listening not only bridge gaps but also heal old wounds in relationships?

Why Listening is More Powerful Than You Think

Active listening is not just a skill; it's an art that, when mastered, can transform the dynamics of any relationship, especially the delicate bond between a parent and child. In the bustling rhythm of daily life, where distractions abound, and communication often becomes transactional, taking the time to truly listen can seem like a luxury. However, this chapter delves into why active listening is crucial in fostering a nurturing environment where children feel genuinely heard and valued.

The essence of active listening lies in *being fully present*. This means setting aside your thoughts and judgments to completely immerse yourself in understanding your child's perspective. It's about hearing beyond the words and grasping the emotions and intentions underlying them. By doing so, you gain insights into your child's inner world and signal to them that their feelings and opinions matter.

Understanding the principles of active listening is foundational. Many misunderstandings in conversations stem from half-listened responses or preconceived interpretations. When parents actively listen, they reduce these miscommunications drastically, paving the way for more effective and heartfelt exchanges. This chapter will explore these principles and underscore their importance in everyday interactions.

Moreover, implementing practices that ensure full presence and empathy might seem challenging amidst our daily routines. Yet, this chapter will provide practical strategies that can be seamlessly integrated into daily interactions with your child. These practices are not about grand gestures but simple habits that can significantly enhance communication quality.

One of active listening's most powerful applications is correcting misunderstandings. Children are still learning to express themselves clearly, and misinterpretations can quickly occur.

Active listening lets parents gently and promptly clarify these ambiguities, reinforcing trust and openness in the relationship.

The ability to engage in active listening also serves as a model for children, teaching them how to listen empathetically to others. This skill is invaluable as it contributes to personal development and building healthier relationships outside the family unit.

This chapter will help you discover how transforming your listening approach can lead to profound changes in your relationship with your child. By embracing the practices discussed here, you will embark on a journey toward creating a more empathetic, understanding, and connected family environment.

Remember, every conversation with your child offers an opportunity to strengthen your bond. The steps outlined in this chapter are designed to improve communication and enrich the emotional landscape shared between you and your child. By mastering the art of being present through active listening, you set the stage for open dialogues that are both healing and empowering.

Active listening is not just about hearing the words spoken; it's about understanding the emotions, intentions, and meanings behind those words. It involves being fully present in the moment, giving undivided attention to the speaker, and showing empathy and non-judgmental understanding. When we actively listen to our children, we create a safe space for them to express themselves openly and honestly. By practicing active listening, we can correct misunderstandings, build trust, and strengthen our bond with our children.

Active listening is crucial in parent-child conversations because it fosters a deeper connection between both parties. Children who feel heard and understood are more likely to communicate openly and honestly. This communication is essential for resolving conflicts, addressing concerns, and nurturing a positive relationship. Active listening goes beyond just nodding; it requires engaging with the speaker, asking clarifying questions, and reflecting on what has been said to ensure mutual understanding.

Empathy plays a significant role in active listening. It involves putting ourselves in our children's shoes, trying to see things from their perspective, and acknowledging their feelings without judgment. When we approach conversations empathetically, we create a supportive environment where our children feel valued and respected. This emotional connection is vital to building trust and strengthening the parent-child relationship over time.

Non-judgmental understanding is another essential aspect of active listening. It involves setting aside our preconceived notions or biases and genuinely listening to what our children say. By suspending judgment, we create a space where our children feel safe expressing their thoughts and emotions without fear of criticism or ridicule. This acceptance fosters honesty and openness in conversations, leading to a deeper trust between parents and children.

Let's explore how you can implement practices that ensure your full presence and empathy during your interactions with your child.

Implementing practices to ensure full presence and empathy during parent-child interactions is vital to fostering a strong and trusting relationship with your child. *Being fully present* means giving your undivided attention when conversing with your child. Put away distractions such as phones or other devices, make eye contact, and show genuine interest in what your child is saying. Doing so creates a safe space for open communication and demonstrates that you value their thoughts and feelings.

Empathy plays a crucial role in active listening. It involves understanding your child's perspective and acknowledging and validating their emotions. When your child expresses their feelings, try to put yourself in their shoes and respond with compassion and understanding. This helps build a sense of connection and trust between you and your child, making them more likely to share openly with you.

Practice reflective listening to show your child you are genuinely engaged in the conversation. Reflective listening involves paraphrasing what your child has said to ensure you have understood correctly. This practice clarifies any potential misunderstandings and demonstrates that you are actively listening and processing their words. It shows your child that their words are valued and respected.

Maintain an open body language during conversations with your child. Non-verbal cues such as facial expressions, gestures, and posture can convey empathy, understanding, and support. Maintaining an open and welcoming stance creates a comfortable environment where your child feels safe expressing themselves without fear of judgment.

Encourage dialogue by asking open-ended questions that invite deeper discussions. Open-ended questions prompt your child to share more than simple yes or no answers, encouraging them to elaborate on their thoughts and feelings. This helps strengthen the bond between you and your child by fostering meaningful conversations that allow for greater understanding and connection.

Avoid interrupting or jumping to conclusions when communicating with your child. Allow them the space to express themselves fully without interjecting or assuming what they are trying to say. By practicing patience and actively listening without interruption, you show respect for your child's voice and encourage them to communicate more openly.

Show empathy through validation by acknowledging your child's emotions without judgment. Let them know that it is okay to feel the way they do, even if you disagree with their perspective.

Validating their feelings creates a supportive atmosphere where they feel understood and accepted, strengthening the parent-child bond.

Incorporating these practices into your interactions with your child can help create a nurturing environment where open communication thrives. By being fully present, showing empathy, practicing reflective listening, maintaining open body language, encouraging dialogue, avoiding interruptions, and validating emotions, you pave the way for meaningful conversations that deepen the connection between you and your child.

Framework: The P.E.A.R.L. Model

Creating a Conducive Environment

To initiate effective active listening, ***creating a conducive environment*** is paramount. This involves setting the stage for open communication by ensuring minimal distractions, choosing an appropriate conversation time, and showing genuine interest in what the child says. By creating a safe and welcoming space, parents signal their readiness to listen attentively.

Demonstrating Physical Attentiveness

Demonstrating physical attentiveness through eye contact, nodding, and open body language is crucial in conveying engagement. These nonverbal cues reassure the child that they have the parent's full focus and encourage them to express themselves openly. Physical attentiveness sets the tone for respectful and meaningful conversations.

· · · ·

UTILIZING VERBAL AFFIRMATIONS and Clarifying Questions

Verbal affirmations and clarifying questions are key components of active listening. Affirmations such as "I see" or "I understand" validate the child's feelings while clarifying questions like "Can you tell me more about that?" demonstrate a genuine interest in understanding their perspective. This back-and-forth dialogue fosters trust and encourages the child to share more openly.

Reflecting on the Child's Feelings

Reflecting on the child's feelings and speech content is essential for accurate understanding. By paraphrasing what the child has said and mirroring their emotions back to them, parents show empathy and validate their experiences. This reflective process deepens the connection and ensures that both parties are on the same page emotionally.

Summarizing and Paraphrasing

Summarizing and paraphrasing help solidify the child's expressed thoughts and feelings. By summarizing key points of the conversation and paraphrasing them back to the child, parents demonstrate comprehension and reinforce the child's sense of being heard. This step ensures clarity and confirms that their message has been received accurately.

Encouraging Continuous Dialogue

Encouraging continuous dialogue through open-ended questions is vital for fostering deeper emotional connections. Open-ended questions invite the child to share more details, thoughts, and feelings, promoting a richer conversation experience. This practice encourages ongoing dialogue, strengthening the parent-child bond over time.

The *P.E.A.R.L. Model* emphasizes a cyclical feedback process between parent and child, where active listening skills are continually honed to enhance understanding and trust within the family unit. Each component is crucial in building strong relationships based on empathy, respect, and effective communication.

Mastering the Heart of Listening: A Step-by-Step Guide

Active listening is more than a skill—it's an essential bridge to deepening trust and understanding in any relationship, particularly between parents and children. This chapter has equipped you with the tools to transform everyday conversations into opportunities for connection and growth. Let's recap the straightforward, actionable steps that can guide you in mastering the art of being present and actively listening to your child.

Step 1: Understanding the Principles of Active Listening

Start by fully immersing yourself in the conversation, focusing intently on your child's words and non-verbal cues. Recognize the importance of giving undivided attention, which signals your child that their thoughts and feelings are valuable.

Step 2: Implementing Practices for Active Listening

Maintain eye contact and avoid interruptions. This shows respect for your child's thoughts and encourages them to express themselves more freely. Utilize affirming nods and verbal acknowledgments to convey your engagement and understanding. By stepping into their shoes, you foster a deeper empathetic connection, crucial for nurturing a supportive dialogue.

Step 3: Using Active Listening to Correct Misunderstandings and Enhance Trust

Misunderstandings are opportunities for clarification and growth. Paraphrase what your child says to ensure mutual understanding, and ask open-ended questions to delve deeper into their thoughts. Your non-judgmental and empathetic responses are crucial to maintaining an open, trusting relationship.

Each step helps resolve misunderstandings and strengthens the emotional bond between you and your child. Incorporating these practices into your daily interactions fosters an environment where open communication thrives, paving the way for a lifetime of strong, understanding relationships.

Remember, mastering active listening is an ongoing journey that requires patience, practice, and a genuine commitment to growth.

As you continue to apply these steps, you'll find that your relationship with your child improves, and your ability to listen actively will enrich all areas of your life. Embrace this journey with an open heart and mind, ready to learn and grow alongside your child.

Chapter 4: Speak Their Language: Tailoring Conversations to Developmental Stages

Can Understanding a Child's World Bridge the Gap?

In the dim light of early morning, Thomas shuffled through the kitchen, his movements slow, burdened with thoughts heavier than the cereal box he pulled from the cupboard. His daughter, Ellie, only eight years old, had been unusually quiet lately. The silence between them grew thicker each day, like fog clinging to a riverbank. He poured milk into her bowl; the white liquid splashed silently against the round curves of cornflakes.

Sitting across from her at the small wooden table that bore witness to countless breakfasts and late-night worries, he noticed how she pushed her food around rather than eating it. Her eyes were distant, lost in some private concern. Thomas knew he needed to reach out to understand her world, which seemed so layered and intricate for someone so young. The challenge was not just in asking what was wrong but in framing his words in a way she could grasp.

Outside, a gentle rain began to tap against the window pane—a rhythmic reminder of nature's persistence. Thomas watched a single droplet trace its path down the glass, merging with others into a tiny creek. "Ellie," he began tentatively, "you know you can tell me anything on your mind, right?" His voice was soft but fraught with concern.

She looked up from her cereal bowl and glanced back down without speaking. He felt the weight of her unspoken words pressing against him. Reflecting on his childhood memories of feeling misunderstood by adults who spoke either over or beneath him stirred a resolve in Thomas to not repeat history.

The room filled with the sound of rain pattering against all that was manufactured and natural outside their cozy kitchen nook. As Ellie played with her spoon, Thomas thought about how children perceive conversations with adults—how direct questions could sometimes feel like towering demands and simple answers could seem like insurmountable puzzles.

He decided then to tell her a story instead of probing further—a story about his own childhood dog, Buster, who always seemed to understand him even when no one else did. As he recounted Buster's antics and unwavering companionship, Ellie's face brightened incrementally, like dawn breaking softly over a sleepy town.

By sharing his vulnerabilities and past joys within stories relatable at her age level, Thomas hoped not just for answers but for an open door into Ellie's world that would invite rather than intrude.

As they shared this momentary connection over childhood pets and playful mischief, Thomas wondered silently if this approach might be what bridges their growing gap—speaking in stories instead of inquiries might turn silent meals into shared narratives.

Could storytelling be our most powerful tool in connecting generations?

Why What You Say Isn't As Important As How You Say It To Your Child

Every parent knows that communication with their child is essential, but not every parent realizes that **their communication** should evolve as their child grows. This chapter delves into the nuances of speaking in a language that matches your child's developmental stage, ensuring your conversations are heard and truly understood.

From the first babbling conversations with toddlers to the more complex dialogues with teenagers, each phase of a child's life requires a different approach to communication. It's not just about what we say—it's about *how* we say it and whether the message is tailored to fit their age and understanding. Aligning our discussions with their emotional and psychological maturity fosters better comprehension and meaningful connections.

The Foundation of Age-Appropriate Communication

Recognizing the importance of age-appropriate communication forms the bedrock of effective parent-child interactions. A toddler might require simple words and plenty of patience. At the same time, teenagers need respect for their growing autonomy and trust assurances. This chapter will explore how these adjustments in our approach can significantly affect how children perceive and respond to us.

Adapting Techniques for Emotional and Cognitive Growth

As children grow, their cognitive abilities and emotional capacities develop rapidly. What was effective last year might not hold their attention or meet their understanding this year. We'll discuss strategies for adapting your conversation techniques to stay in sync with these changes, ensuring that your bond strengthens even as they evolve.

Measuring Success in Communication

Finally, assessing the effectiveness of these tailored communication strategies is vital. Are our messages getting through? Do our children feel heard and understood? We will look at ways to evaluate the impact of our adjusted communication methods across different ages and stages, providing you with tools to continuously improve how you connect with your child.

By embracing these principles, parents can transform potential misunderstandings into opportunities for growth and deeper connection. Each conversation becomes a building block in a lifelong bond, teaching us as much about ourselves as it does about our children. This chapter aims to equip you with the understanding necessary to navigate this complex yet rewarding aspect of parenting.

Through thoughtful adaptation and careful assessment, we can ensure that our conversations are developmentally appropriate and profoundly impactful. Let's embark on this journey together, learning to speak not just to our children but directly to their hearts.

Age-appropriate communication is not just a nicety but a necessity for fostering meaningful connections with children. Understanding a child's developmental stages is crucial in tailoring conversations that resonate with their emotional and cognitive maturity. Each stage of a child's growth comes with unique characteristics that influence how they perceive and process information. By recognizing these differences, parents can adapt their communication style to meet the child where they are, creating a bridge for effective dialogue.

Recognizing the importance of age-appropriate communication means acknowledging that what works for one age group may not work for another. For example, toddlers require simple language and concrete examples to grasp concepts. At the same time, teenagers are more inclined towards abstract thinking and complex discussions. Failure to adjust communication styles based on these developmental disparities can lead to misunderstandings, frustration, and disconnection between parent and child.

Understanding the significance of age-appropriate conversations is about more than talking down to children or oversimplifying complex topics. *It is about meeting them at their level* and engaging them in ways that make sense to their evolving minds. By tailoring conversations to match their developmental stage, parents create an environment where children feel understood, respected, and valued.

Adapting communication techniques to match a child's emotional and cognitive maturity involves being attuned to their needs and capabilities. Infants respond to soothing tones and facial expressions, while preschoolers thrive on repetition and interactive play. As children grow older, their cognitive abilities expand, allowing for more in-depth discussions on values, emotions, and relationships.

By adjusting the tone, content, and delivery of conversations according to these developmental milestones, parents can ensure that their children hear and internalize their messages.

In essence, age-appropriate communication is not a one-size-fits-all approach but a tailored strategy that evolves alongside the child's growth. *It requires flexibility*, patience, and an understanding of the unique characteristics of each developmental stage. By recognizing the importance of age-appropriate conversations, parents lay the foundation for building strong, trusting relationships with their children based on mutual respect and effective dialogue.

Continue reading to explore how adapting conversation techniques can strengthen parent-child bonds by aligning with various developmental stages.

Adapting conversation techniques to match a child's emotional and cognitive maturity is a crucial aspect of effective communication.

Understanding where a child is developmentally allows parents to tailor their conversations in ways that resonate with them. *By aligning communication styles with the child's growth stage, parents can ensure that their messages are heard and understood.*

For younger children, such as toddlers or preschoolers, using simple language and concrete examples can help convey ideas effectively. *Being mindful of their limited attention span and ability to grasp abstract concepts is essential in fostering clear communication.*

As children grow older into elementary school, conversations can become more nuanced and detailed. Parents should be prepared to engage in discussions that encourage critical thinking and curiosity while maintaining simplicity in their explanations. *Encouraging questions and providing patient answers can foster a sense of trust and openness between parent and child.* During these formative years, children develop their sense of self and understanding of the world around them, making it a suitable time for meaningful dialogues.

Communication takes on a new level of complexity when dealing with teenagers. Adolescents are navigating intense emotional growth and self-discovery, which can often lead to heightened sensitivity and resistance to authority figures. *Parents should approach conversations with teens with empathy, respect, and a willingness to listen without judgment.* Acknowledging their autonomy while providing guidance can help build mutual respect and understanding.

Adapting communication techniques to suit the child's developmental stage fosters a healthy environment for open dialogue. It allows conversations to flow more naturally, with both parties feeling heard and valued. *By recognizing children's unique needs and capabilities at different ages, parents can create a foundation for strong, trusting relationships built on effective communication.* This adaptability in communication styles showcases a parent's commitment to understanding and connecting with their child on a deeper level, ultimately nurturing a bond that withstands the tests of time and development.

When assessing the effectiveness of communication strategies tailored to different developmental stages, it becomes evident that flexibility and understanding are paramount in fostering meaningful dialogues with children. Each stage of development presents unique challenges and opportunities for communication.

Observing and adjusting our approach to match the child's emotional and cognitive maturity is crucial for successful interactions. Being attuned to the child's needs and abilities can create a more supportive environment for conversations to thrive.

One key aspect in evaluating communication strategies is the child's responsiveness. When a child is engaged, responsive, and actively participating in conversations, the approach resonates with them. *Encouraging an open dialogue* where children feel comfortable expressing themselves is a positive sign of effective communication techniques. *Listening attentively* to their responses and reactions can provide valuable insights into how well they understand and engage with the conversation.

Another vital factor to consider when assessing communication strategies is the message's clarity. It is essential to ensure that our words are age-appropriate, understandable, and relevant to the child's developmental stage. *Using simple language,* providing context when needed, and checking for comprehension can help maintain clarity in communication. *Avoiding jargon or complex terminology that* may confuse or overwhelm the child is vital to effective conversations.

Feedback from children can also serve as a valuable indicator of the success of our communication strategies. Children may offer cues through their body language, facial expressions, or verbal responses that signal whether they are engaged or struggling to follow along. *Being receptive* to these cues and adjusting our approach accordingly can enhance the quality of communication and strengthen the parent-child bond.

Reflecting on the outcomes of conversations with children at different developmental stages allows us to refine our communication skills over time. We can continuously adapt our strategies to better meet the child's evolving needs by evaluating what worked well and what could be improved upon. *Learning from each interaction* helps us grow as communicators and fosters a deeper connection with our children.

In conclusion, assessing the effectiveness of communication strategies adapted to various developmental stages involves keen observation, active listening, clarity in messaging, receptivity to feedback, and a commitment to continuous improvement. By staying attuned to the child's cues and adjusting our approach accordingly, we can cultivate meaningful conversations that nurture understanding and strengthen relationships with our children.

Recognizing the importance of age-appropriate conversations in mastering the art of family communication cannot be overstated. By adapting our dialogue to align with our children's emotional and cognitive maturity, we open the door to more meaningful and effective interactions. This chapter has underscored how critical it is to tailor our communication strategies to suit the developmental stages of our children, ensuring that our messages are heard and fully understood.

Age-appropriate communication is the cornerstone of building a robust and enduring bond with our children. When we speak in a way that resonates with their level of understanding, we foster a sense of security and trust. This connection paves the way for open and honest dialogue, essential as they grow and encounter various challenges.

Adapting our conversation techniques requires a keen observation and understanding of our child's current capabilities and emotional state. This thoughtful approach enables us to guide them through their feelings and thoughts in a supportive manner. By assessing the effectiveness of our adapted communication strategies, we ensure that we are continually meeting their evolving needs.

It's important to remember that this process is not static. As our children grow, so too must our strategies evolve. Parenting is a journey of constant learning and adaptation. By committing to this dynamic approach, we support our children's development and deepen our relationship with them.

Let us carry this knowledge and commitment into every conversation with our children. By doing so, we enhance our day-to-day interactions and lay the groundwork for a lifetime of open communication and mutual understanding. Herein lies the potential to transform everyday misunderstandings into opportunities for growth and deeper connection.

As we continue through this book, let's remember the power of speaking from the heart in ways that our children can truly grasp. This approach will not only enrich our family life but also empower our children to navigate the world with confidence and clarity.

Chapter 5: Beyond Words: The Significance of Non-Verbal Cues

How Well Can Silence Speak?

Margaret watched her son, Jamie, from across the kitchen table.

The morning sun filtered through the window, casting long shadows on his downturned face. His spoon clinked against the cereal bowl rhythmically, a mundane sound that seemed louder in the thick silence between them. She noticed his furrowed brow and how his lips turned down slightly at the corners.

Last night's argument hung heavy in the air, an invisible yet palpable weight that pressed down on both their shoulders. They had argued about his late nights out, and she had tried to explain her worries with words that felt both sharp and inadequate. Now, in the quiet of a new day, she wondered if her facial expressions and tone had conveyed more concern and love than her actual words.

The room was cool but filled with slants of warmth from the sunbeams. Outside, a dog barked, momentarily breaking Margaret's train of thought. She glanced outside; Mrs. Thompson slowly walked her old Labrador down the street. The dog moved with difficulty, but there was no mistaking the understanding between him and his owner.

Back inside, Jamie shifted, pushing away his half-eaten breakfast. His movements spoke volumes; they were quick and restless compared to last night's languid defiance.

Margaret tentatively reached across the table, placing her hand near his arm without touching him—her gesture a silent plea for reconciliation. She remembered how he reached for her hand when he was younger whenever clouds darkened his mood.

Jamie looked up then, meeting her eyes for the first time that morning. His gaze held a mix of adolescent confusion and nascent understanding—a silent acknowledgment of their regret over last night's harsh words.

As he stood to clear his bowl to the sink, Margaret noticed how tall he had become. He no longer seemed to fit into the framework of her little boy, who needed comforting cuddles and sweet words alone.

She sipped her coffee slowly and watched him rinse off his dish under running water—the sound crisp in their quiet kitchen. He didn't slam things around as might be expected after an argument; instead, there was a carefulness to his movements that softened something inside her.

In this slice of everyday life, a question unspoken but hanging between them like ripe fruit—could they learn to speak less with their mouths and more with their hearts? And amidst these silent exchanges laden with meaning, could silence speak louder than words?

The Silent Symphony of Parenting

Words often take center stage in the intricate dance of parent-child relationships. Still, the unspoken signals orchestrate much of the emotional and psychological connection. This chapter delves into the profound impact of nonverbal communication within family dynamics, exploring how subtle cues can significantly influence interactions and relationships. As parents, understanding and mastering these silent messages is crucial in nurturing a secure, empathetic environment conducive to open conversations and deep connections.

Non-verbal communication encompasses everything from facial expressions and body language to tone of voice and physical proximity. These elements convey emotions and intentions sometimes more powerfully than words could ever do. With their keen observational skills, children are particularly sensitive to these cues, often picking up on inconsistencies between what is said and silently expressed.

This sensitivity can be a double-edged sword. On one hand, it helps children develop empathy and understand complex emotional landscapes. On the other hand, it can lead to confusion if parents' words do not align with their non-verbal messages. Thus, *the congruence between verbal and non-verbal communication* becomes essential in fostering trust and clarity.

Understanding Without Words

Imagine a scenario where a parent verbally encourages their child's efforts in schoolwork but wears a frown or maintains a closed body posture. The mixed signals can leave the child uncertain about the genuine sentiment, potentially undermining the verbal encouragement. This chapter will explore how parents can become more aware of their non-verbal signals and learn to manage them effectively to support their verbal messages.

Decoding Children's Silent Speech

Children are not always able to articulate their thoughts and feelings verbally. Instead, they often rely on nonverbal modes to express themselves. Whether a toddler throws toys to show frustration or a teenager rolls their eyes, each action carries a wealth of information about their internal state. By learning to decode these signals, parents can respond more appropriately to their children's needs and emotions, thus avoiding escalations of conflicts and misunderstandings.

Aligning Words with Actions

The alignment of verbal and non-verbal communication is pivotal in maintaining clear communication. When parents consistently match their body language with their words, children receive coherent messages, reducing anxiety and confusion. This chapter will provide practical strategies for parents to enhance their awareness of their body language while aligning it closely with their spoken words.

Through this exploration of non-verbal cues within the parent-child dynamic, we aim to equip parents with the skills to enhance understanding and empathy in conversations with their children. By focusing on these silent yet powerful aspects of communication, parents can foster deeper connections, encourage more open dialogue, and build stronger bonds that withstand the tests of time and challenge.

Understanding non-verbal cues goes beyond mere observation; it involves an intuitive leap into interpreting and appropriately responding to those cues for better relationship outcomes. This chapter sets the stage for parents who wish to master this less visible yet impactful communication realm as part of nurturing a fulfilling relationship with their children.

Nonverbal communication is pivotal in parent-child interactions, often speaking volumes without needing words. How we hold ourselves, our facial expressions and even our silence can convey emotions and messages that may not be articulated verbally. *These nonverbal cues are particularly significant in the parent-child dynamic,* as children are highly attuned to their parents' subtle signals. A furrowed brow, a gentle smile, or a comforting touch can communicate love, understanding, or concern far more powerfully than words alone.

Parents must recognize the impact of their non-verbal communication, as it can either reinforce or contradict their verbal messages. For instance, saying "I'm proud of you" while looking distracted or disinterested sends conflicting signals to a child.

Inconsistencies between verbal and non-verbal cues can lead to confusion and misunderstanding, potentially eroding trust and connection over time. Therefore, being mindful of one's body language, facial expressions, and gestures is crucial in fostering effective communication with children.

Children often rely on non-verbal cues to interpret the emotional landscape around them. They may pick up on subtle shifts in their parents' demeanor, sensing tension or relaxation even before any words are spoken. In this way, *non-verbal communication serves as an unspoken dialogue between parent and child,* shaping the emotional atmosphere of their interactions. By being aware of the messages they convey through non-verbal means, parents can create a more nurturing and supportive environment for their children to thrive.

Nonverbal cues can also provide insights into a child's emotional state, offering clues about their feelings and needs when they struggle to express them verbally. A downturned gaze crossed arms, or fidgeting could indicate a child's discomfort, anxiety, or resistance. *By attuning themselves to these nonverbal signals,* parents can better understand their child's inner world and respond with empathy and support.

Discovering the nuances of non-verbal communication is vital to fostering deeper connections with your child.

Paying attention to verbal and nonverbal cues in your interactions can help you have a more harmonious and understanding relationship with your child.

Non-verbal communication is a powerful tool in understanding children's emotions and thoughts. While words can convey explicit messages, non-verbal cues often reveal the underlying feelings that words may not express. *Body language, facial expressions, tone of voice, and even periods of silence* play crucial roles in deciphering what a child genuinely tries to communicate. As parents, we must pay close attention to these non-verbal signals to gain a deeper insight into our children's inner worlds.

Children may not always articulate their emotions verbally, especially when young or facing complex feelings. In such cases, their nonverbal cues become the primary means of expression. *A furrowed brow, fidgeting hands, or avoiding eye contact can* speak volumes about a child's state of mind. Parents can better understand their children's needs and provide appropriate support and guidance by learning to decode these signals.

One key aspect of decoding non-verbal cues is observing consistency or inconsistency between verbal and non-verbal messages. Children may say one thing but convey different emotions through body language. For example, a child might say they are okay while crossing their arms and avoiding eye contact, indicating discomfort or distress. **Parents** can initiate conversations that delve deeper into the child's feelings and concerns by noting these discrepancies.

Understanding non-verbal cues also involves being attuned to context. A child's body language can vary significantly based on stress, fatigue, or excitement. *By considering the broader context*, parents can better interpret non-verbal signals and respond appropriately to their child's emotional needs.

Empathy plays a crucial role in interpreting nonverbal cues.

Putting oneself in the child's shoes and imagining how they might feel can enhance one's ability to understand nonverbal communication effectively. *Empathy fosters more profound connections* between parents and children, creating an environment where open dialogue and emotional expression are encouraged.

Non-verbal cues often provide valuable insights into unspoken thoughts and emotions, allowing parents to address underlying issues children may struggle to verbally articulate. By honing the decoding of these cues, parents can build stronger bonds with their children based on mutual understanding and empathy. *Being mindful of verbal and non-verbal communication is essential for fostering clear, honest dialogues* that nurture trust and emotional connection within the parent-child relationship.

In essence, learning to decode and understand the non-verbal cues children use is a vital skill for effective communication. Parents can gain profound insights into their children's emotions and thoughts by paying attention to body language, facial expressions, tone of voice, and contextual factors. *Consistency between verbal and non-verbal messages,* empathy towards the child's experiences, and an awareness of the broader context all enhance communication dynamics within the family unit. Through this understanding, parents can create an environment where emotions are acknowledged, conversations are meaningful, and relationships flourish based on mutual respect and understanding.

Non-verbal cues play a crucial role in communication, often complementing or contradicting our words. To ensure effective communication with our children, we must align our verbal and non-verbal messages to prevent confusion and misinterpretation.

Maintaining clarity in communication requires consistency between what we say and how we express ourselves non-verbally.

Children are perceptive, picking up on subtle cues that adults may not even know they are sending. Therefore, as parents, we must be mindful of our body language, facial expressions, and overall demeanor when interacting with our children.

Children may become confused or distrustful of the communication exchange when verbal and non-verbal messages are incongruent. For instance, saying "I'm fine" with a frown on your face can send mixed signals to your child. They might sense that something is wrong despite your words suggesting otherwise.

Consistency in verbal and non-verbal cues fosters trust and understanding in parent-child relationships. It creates a safe space for open communication where children feel confident expressing their thoughts and emotions without fear of misinterpretation.

Body language is a powerful nonverbal communication tool, often conveying emotions more honestly than words. *Simple actions like maintaining eye contact, nodding in agreement, or using open gestures can reinforce the message you are trying to convey verbally.* Conversely, crossing your arms, avoiding eye contact, or fidgeting can signal defensiveness or discomfort, leading to a breakdown in communication. *Being aware of your body language allows you to intentionally align it with your words,* enhancing the clarity and impact of your message.

Facial expressions also play a significant role in non-verbal communication. A smile instantly conveys warmth and acceptance, while a furrowed brow might indicate concern or disapproval. *Children are highly attuned to facial cues,* often interpreting them instinctively without conscious thought. By ensuring that your facial expressions match the content of your conversation, you create an environment where emotional authenticity thrives. *Consistent verbal and non-verbal messages build emotional connections and strengthen bonds between parents and children.*

Silence is another form of nonverbal communication that holds great significance. Silence can sometimes speak volumes, conveying emotions that words cannot capture. *However, prolonged silence or avoidance of discussion can also lead to misunderstandings.* It is essential to strike a balance between verbal expression and moments of silence, using pauses purposefully to allow for reflection or information processing. *Parents* can create a conversation rhythm that promotes active listening and deeper understanding by aligning verbal statements with intentional periods of silence.

In essence, *effective communication hinges on aligning verbal and non-verbal messages.* Consistency in tone, body language, facial expressions, and use of silence enhances the clarity of our interactions with children. *We* cultivate trust, understanding, and emotional connection with our children by consciously integrating these elements into our conversations. *The harmonious blend of verbal and non-verbal cues paves the way for meaningful dialogues that nurture healthy relationships* built on mutual respect and genuine communication.

As we wrap up our exploration of nonverbal cues in parent-child interactions, we must recognize the profound impact these silent signals have on our communication. Nonverbal communication—encompassing everything from a subtle brow furrow to the comfort of a gentle touch—plays a pivotal role in how we connect and understand each other, especially in the dynamic between parents and children.

Understanding and interpreting these cues accurately is not just beneficial but essential. It allows parents to respond more effectively to their children's unspoken needs and emotions. This responsiveness fosters a deeper emotional connection and enhances mutual trust and understanding.

Moreover, aligning verbal expressions with non-verbal cues is vital. When what we say matches how we say it, we reduce the chances of misunderstandings and conflicts. This alignment reassures children, providing a sense of consistency and security crucial for their emotional development.

Being more aware of the non-verbal messages we send and receive opens up new avenues for empathy and connection. This awareness is not just about better communication; it's about building stronger, more resilient relationships that can withstand parenting challenges.

As we move forward, remember that our body language, facial expressions, and silence speak volumes. Let's commit to being as transparent and harmonious in our silent messages as our spoken words, enhancing every interaction with our children.

Through attentive practice and mindful interaction, we become not only better communicators but also role models for our children for the importance of empathy, understanding, and emotional intelligence. These invaluable lessons equip them with skills that transcend the confines of family life, preparing them for a lifetime of meaningful relationships.

Let us embrace the power of non-verbal communication to transform our conversations and connections with our children, ensuring that every gesture and glance contributes positively to our shared journey of growth and understanding.

Chapter 6: Navigating Sensitive Waters: Discussing Difficult Topics with Ease

How Does One Navigate the Choppy Waters of a Child's Awakening?

Morning light crept through the blinds, casting long stripes across the kitchen table where Michael sat, his fingers drumming on the wood. The coffee in his mug had cooled to an undrinkable tepidity, forgotten amid his spiraling thoughts. Today was the day he had decided to talk to his son, Jamie, about some of the harsher realities of life—those sensitive topics that lurk in every parent's periphery until they force themselves to the center.

Outside, a light breeze stirred the oak tree leaves that shadowed their small backyard. Michael watched as a single leaf detached and fluttered down—a slow, meandering dance before it settled on the moist earth. It was autumn, and with it came changes, not just in nature but within their home. Jamie had recently faced bullying at school over a misunderstood comment about personal beliefs. The incident had left him confused and hurt, retreating into a shell that even his parents seemed unable to reach.

Michael's mind wandered back to his youth—the struggles and confrontations he had endured and how little guidance he had received from anyone around him. He remembered feeling lost, wishing for someone to steer him right or listen without judgment. This memory fueled his resolve; he wouldn't let Jamie flounder through these formative years alone.

The sound of footsteps snapped Michael out of his reverie. Jamie entered the kitchen, tousled hair shadowing puzzled eyes as he noticed his father's serious demeanor. "Dad? Is everything okay?" he asked as he reached for an apple from the bowl on the counter.

"Sit down with me for a minute," Michael gestured towards the chair beside him. His voice held a calmness that belied the tumult inside him. As Jamie sat, looking expectant yet apprehensive, Michael searched for honest yet protective words. How do you explain societal complexities to an eleven-year-old without painting too grim a picture?

They talked about school first—mundane things that led them gently into deeper waters. Michael watched Jamie's expressions shift from curiosity to concern when they touched upon diversity and empathy toward others' feelings and beliefs.

"Sometimes people fear what they don't understand," Michael explained softly, hoping to sow seeds of tolerance in fertile young soil. "And sometimes that fear can make them unkind or unfair."

Jamie nodded slowly, understanding—or at least beginning to understand—the layers beneath people's actions.

A car honked outside, briefly pulling their attention away from their cocoon of dialogue—a reminder that life went on around them relentlessly.

As they resumed talking, Michael felt this moment swell with significance—the kind that shapes character and cement bonds. He could only hope that these discussions would forge in Jamie resilience and wisdom beyond his years.

In moments like these—fraught with potential yet brimming with vulnerability—one wonders how many such conversations are happening across homes worldwide? How many parents are navigating these turbulent waters right now?

The Delicate Dance of Dialogue

Broaching sensitive topics with our children is manageable in terms of parenting. Whether we're discussing the complexities of relationships, the challenges of mental health, or the intricacies of societal issues, the way we initiate and navigate these conversations can significantly impact our children's emotional well-being. *It is essential to approach these dialogues with tact, understanding, and a strategy that fosters trust and openness.*

The Art of Introduction

Introducing sensitive subjects is not just about what we say but how we say it. The initial approach can set the tone for the entire conversation. Parents must be equipped with techniques that ease into these topics gently and respectfully, ensuring that children feel safe and valued. We can open avenues for deeper understanding and connection by carefully choosing our words and timing.

Creating a Safe Space

Conversation about a tricky topic requires a secure and private environment. This chapter will explore how to create a space where children know that their thoughts and feelings are welcomed and protected. This involves physical privacy and an emotional assurance that their disclosures will be met with support and empathy.

Unconditional Support: The Foundation

At the heart of effective communication lies unconditional support. When children feel supported regardless of their views or feelings, they are more likely to express themselves honestly and openly. This chapter will explore how parents can consistently reinforce their support, clarifying that the child's value is not tied to their opinions or emotions.

Navigating sensitive topics requires more than good intentions; it demands a deliberate strategy that respects both the child's perspective and the parent's concern. The techniques discussed in this chapter aim to equip parents with tools to manage these difficult conversations and transform them into opportunities for growth and connection.

Empathy plays a crucial role in all this. Understanding your child's viewpoint is pivotal in addressing any sensitive issue effectively. Reflecting on our own experiences while respecting their unique perspective fosters a two-way dialogue characterized by mutual respect.

Finally, resilience should be woven through every discussion on sensitive topics. Teaching our children, by example, how to handle life's difficulties with grace is perhaps one of the most valuable lessons they can learn from these conversations.

By mastering these communicative strategies, parents can ensure that tough talks don't just end with understanding but also enhance the trust and bond within the family, paving the way for future dialogues. These conversations are not just about addressing immediate concerns but are stepping stones toward nurturing a lifelong, open, and honest relationship.

Your approach can significantly impact the conversation's outcome when discussing sensitive topics with your children. Developing techniques for introducing and discussing these subjects is crucial in creating a safe and open space for communication. *Choosing the right moment* to broach a complex topic can set the tone for the entire discussion. It's essential to pick a time when you and your child are relaxed and free from distractions, allowing for a more focused and meaningful exchange.

Setting the stage for these conversations involves creating an environment of trust and understanding. *Approaching the topic with empathy* and a non-confrontational attitude can help ease any tension or apprehension your child may feel. By demonstrating that you are there to listen without judgment, you create a space where they feel comfortable expressing their thoughts and emotions openly.

Using age-appropriate language is another crucial aspect of discussing sensitive subjects with children. Tailoring your language to suit their level of understanding ensures that they grasp the topic easily. *Encouraging questions* and being prepared to provide honest answers can foster a sense of transparency and encourage further dialogue on the subject.

Active listening is a fundamental skill when discussing sensitive topics. By giving your full attention to your child's words, you show them that their thoughts and feelings are valued. *Reflecting* on what they have shared demonstrates that you understand their perspective, fostering deeper connections and building trust in the relationship.

Creating an atmosphere where your child feels safe to express themselves is essential for navigating difficult conversations successfully. *You* lay the foundation for constructive dialogues that strengthen your bond with your child by approaching these topics with sensitivity, empathy, and openness. Remember, every conversation is an opportunity for growth and understanding in your parent-child relationship.

Continue reading to learn how to establish a secure and private environment conducive to open conversations on challenging topics.

Establishing a secure and private environment for discussing sensitive topics with your children is crucial for fostering open and honest conversations. *Creating a safe space* where your child feels comfortable sharing their thoughts and feelings can make all the difference in how these discussions unfold. *Privacy is vital*, allowing your child to speak freely without fear of judgment or outside interference. Find a quiet and secluded setting where you can talk without distractions, ensuring your child feels heard and respected.

Offering reassurance and unconditional support is essential in building trust during these conversations. Let your child know that they can express themselves without facing negative consequences. *Listening attentively and showing empathy for* their emotions can help them feel validated and understood. Your role as a parent is to provide guidance and be a supportive presence that encourages openness and honesty.

Encouraging active listening during these discussions is vital for creating a safe space. Show genuine interest in your child's words, ask clarifying questions, and reflect on their feelings to ensure you understand them correctly. ***Demonstrate empathy*** by acknowledging their emotions, even if you may not fully agree with their perspective. By actively engaging in the conversation, you show your child that their thoughts are valued and respected.

Maintaining confidentiality is another critical aspect of creating a secure environment for discussing sensitive topics. Assure your child that what they share with you will remain between the two of you unless there are concerns about their safety or well-being.

Respecting their privacy builds trust and encourages them to confide in you without hesitation.

In summary, establishing a secure and private environment for discussing challenging topics with your children involves ***creating a safe space, offering unconditional support, encouraging active listening,*** and ***maintaining confidentiality.*** By prioritizing these elements, you can cultivate trust and openness, allowing meaningful conversations on sensitive subjects.

Foster an atmosphere of unconditional support to encourage honesty and openness.

Creating an environment of unconditional support within the family is paramount for fostering honest and open communication. ***Parents can encourage their children to express themselves freely without fear of judgment or repercussions*** by offering unwavering support. This supportive atmosphere instills confidence in children, allowing them to share their thoughts and feelings openly, even on challenging topics.

Listening without interruption and showing genuine empathy towards your child's concerns are crucial to providing unconditional support. By actively listening, parents convey that their child's feelings are valid and respected, creating a safe space where discussions can thrive. Additionally, offering reassurance that their emotions are understood and accepted helps build trust and strengthens the parent-child bond.

Avoiding criticism or dismissive responses is critical to maintaining a supportive environment. Children need to feel they can confide in their parents without fear of being judged or belittled. By refraining from harsh judgments or quick dismissals, parents pave the way for meaningful conversations that promote honesty and trust.

Demonstrating empathy through understanding and validation can significantly impact how children perceive their ability to communicate openly. Empathy shows children that their parents care about their feelings and are willing to support them unconditionally. This validation encourages children to share their thoughts honestly, knowing they will be met with understanding and compassion.

Encouraging openness through active conversation engagement is a powerful way to foster trust and honesty within the family unit. By actively participating in discussions, parents show interest in their children's perspectives, reinforcing that their opinions are valued. *This active engagement creates a sense of inclusivity and mutual respect, nurturing an environment where honesty can flourish.*

Embracing vulnerability and sharing personal experiences can also help cultivate an atmosphere of unconditional support within the family. When parents open up about their struggles or challenges, it humanizes the conversation, making it easier for children to relate and feel comfortable sharing their experiences.

This vulnerability fosters a deeper connection between parent and child, leading to more authentic and meaningful conversations.

In conclusion, fostering an atmosphere of unconditional support within the family is essential for encouraging honesty and openness in discussions on sensitive topics. *By providing unwavering support, active listening, empathy, avoiding criticism, demonstrating engagement, and embracing vulnerability*, parents can create a safe space where children feel valued, understood, and free to express themselves honestly. This supportive environment strengthens the parent-child bond and lays the foundation for healthy communication dynamics within the family.

Navigating sensitive topics with your children is not just about the discussion itself but also about how you approach these conversations. The techniques and environments you create are foundational to fostering trust and openness in your family dynamics.

Step-by-Step Guide: "Heartfelt Conversations"

Objective: The goal of "Heartfelt Conversations" is to equip parents with practical, actionable steps to effectively discuss sensitive topics with their children. This process strengthens the parent-child relationship by ensuring these discussions are approached with empathy, privacy, and unconditional support.

1. *Developing Techniques for Introducing Sensitive Subjects*

○ Start by choosing an appropriate time and place, ensuring the setting is private and distractions-free. Initiating these discussions is crucial when you and your child feel calm and unpressured.

○ Use a calm and non-confrontational tone immediately to convey sensitivity and understanding. This approach helps set a tone of safety and openness.

○ *Timeframe:* Allow 10-15 minutes to plan your approach, considering the best time and setting to talk.

1. *Establishing a Secure and Private Environment for Open Conversations*

○ Create a safe and welcoming space where your child knows their thoughts and feelings are valued. Reassure them that they are in a supportive environment.

○ Avoid negative reactions to their disclosures. Respond instead with empathy and strive to understand their perspective fully.

○ *Timeframe*: This step is ongoing; continuously strive to maintain and reinforce this environment in all interactions.

1. *Fostering an Atmosphere of Unconditional Support*

- Communicate openly that your love and support are unwavering, regardless of the conversation's content. Use affirming statements like, "I'm glad you trusted me enough to share this with me," or "I love you no matter what."

- Ensure your responses validate their feelings, avoiding any dismissal of their experiences.

- *Timeframe:* This is also an ongoing practice that should be evident in daily interactions.

Evaluating Success:

To gauge the effectiveness of these steps, observe if your child seems more willing to engage in conversations over time. Feedback can be direct through their expressions of comfort or indirectly noticed through their willingness to initiate sensitive discussions.

• • • •

BY IMPLEMENTING THESE steps, you create a framework

within which sensitive topics can be explored safely and constructively. Remember, the essence of these conversations lies not just in the issues discussed but profoundly in how they are conducted. Your approach can significantly influence your child's willingness to share and strengthen your family's trust and bond.

Chapter 7: Rituals of Connection: Establishing Consistent Communication Patterns

Can Rituals Bridge the Gap?

In the quiet glow of the evening, as golden hues melted into shadows across the suburban landscape, Sarah walked alongside her ten-year-old son, Jamie. Their post-dinner ritual was more than a walk; it was a silent pact of sharing and unburdening. The air was crisp, carrying whispers of winter's approach, and rustling leaves underfoot accompanied their steps.

Jamie's usually bright eyes held a heaviness today. Sarah noticed but waited. The beauty of their ritual lay in its patience and predictability; it gave Jamie the security to open up on his terms. She could almost hear his thoughts tumbling like the pebbles beneath the water's surface as they turned down the path alongside the gently murmuring creek.

Suddenly, Jamie stopped and looked up at his mother. "Mom, why do people stop talking to each other?" His voice was small against the vastness of twilight. The question stemmed from a day at school where friendships seemed as fragile as morning dew.

Sarah's heart clenched softly, her mind racing back to her childhood memories filled with similar fears and confusions. She knelt beside him, her jeans soaking up the damp earth's scent. "Sometimes," she began, choosing her words with care akin to picking stepping stones across this creek, "people need time or space to understand themselves better before they can share with others again." She touched his hand lightly—a leaf brushing against the skin—reassuring in its fleeting contact.

They resumed walking, Jamie processing her words while absently kicking at fallen acorns that dotted their path. Sarah reflected on how these walks opened doors between them that daily routines otherwise kept shut. Each step seemed an affirmation—a silent declaration that here in this space, they were both present for each other.

As night drew its curtain tighter around them and stars blinked awake above, Sarah wondered what thoughts wandered through Jamie's young mind, now stirred by their talk ritual. Would these moments be enough to guide him through life's inevitable silences?

Could establishing such simple rituals be key in nurturing lifelong openness?

Transforming Everyday Moments into Meaningful Conversations

Establishing a 'Talk Ritual' might seem simple, but its impact on family communication is profound. At the heart of effective parenting is the ability to foster open lines of communication with children, ensuring they feel heard, valued, and understood. This chapter delves into how regularizing communication through specific rituals can create a nurturing environment conducive to open dialogue and emotional security.

The Power of Predictability in Communication

Consistency is critical to building trust and comfort in any relationship, especially between parents and children. Parents send a clear message by setting aside dedicated time and conversation spaces: *"I am here for you."* This predictability eases children's anxieties and empowers them to share their thoughts and feelings more freely. They grow up knowing that there are specific times when they have their parent's undivided attention, which can be incredibly reassuring.

Setting the Stage for Open Dialogues

Establishing these rituals does not require grand gestures. Instead, it's about integrating them seamlessly into daily routines—be it a nightly chat before bedtime or a walk after dinner. Each family's ritual will look different, tailored to their unique dynamics and schedules. However, the intention behind these rituals remains universal: to cultivate an environment where children feel safe to express themselves without fear of judgment or dismissal.

The Benefits Unfold

The benefits of such structured communication extend beyond just having conversations; they lay the foundation for developing emotional intelligence and resilience in children. Regular interactions focused on their day-to-day experiences teach them how to articulate their emotions, handle interpersonal relationships, and navigate life's ups and downs. Over time, these moments of connection accumulate, significantly strengthening the parent-child bond.

Creating a Culture of Communication

This chapter will explore how parents can effectively initiate and maintain these communication rituals. It will provide practical advice on choosing the right time and setting that aligns with parent and child needs, ensuring that these conversations become a cherished part of their routine rather than a chore. Moreover, it will highlight how these consistent practices can adapt as children grow older and their needs evolve.

The Long-Term Impact

By committing to these communication practices, parents lay the groundwork for their children to develop into confident individuals who feel secure in expressing themselves. This long-term investment in fostering open communication channels benefits the child and the entire family's relational dynamics.

In navigating through this chapter, readers will gain insights into establishing these rituals and understanding their profound impact on family life. The journey towards mastering the art of family communication begins with simple steps that promise to transform misunderstandings into opportunities for growth and deeper connection.

Regular communication patterns with your child is crucial for building a solid and lasting bond. ***Setting up 'Talk Rituals' can be a powerful way to ensure consistent and meaningful conversations.*** By designating a specific time and place for these interactions, you create a reliable environment where your child feels secure in sharing their thoughts and emotions.

'Talk Rituals' can take many forms. It could be a nightly chat before bedtime, a walk after dinner, or even a dedicated time during the weekend. The key is establishing a routine that works for you and your child, ensuring you have uninterrupted time to connect and communicate.

These rituals signal your child that you are available and interested in their day-to-day experiences. They provide a sense of security and comfort, knowing there is a designated time to share what's on their mind without any distractions. Over time, this consistency can deepen your relationship and foster open communication between you and your child.

When setting up 'Talk Rituals,' it's essential to be present and fully engaged during these conversations. Put away distractions such as phones or laptops, and give your child your undivided attention. Show genuine interest in what they say, ask open-ended questions, and listen actively to their responses. This level of attentiveness demonstrates to your child that their thoughts and feelings are valued.

Consistent communication patterns help establish trust between you and your child. When they know they can count on you to listen and engage with them regularly, they are more likely to open up about their struggles, successes, fears, and dreams. This trust forms the foundation of a solid parent-child relationship built on mutual respect and understanding.

Regularizing communication through 'Talk Rituals' creates a safe space for your child to express themselves. This predictability makes them comfortable sharing even the most difficult or sensitive topics with you. As a parent, being present during these conversations shows your child that you are there to support them unconditionally.

Ready to explore the benefits of consistent communication spaces further? Keep reading to learn how nightly chats or post-dinner walks can transform your parent-child relationship.

Consistent communication spaces, such as nightly chats or post-dinner walks, offer many benefits for parents and children. *These rituals create a dedicated time and place for open dialogue, fostering a sense of security and trust in the relationship.* By regularly engaging in these conversations, parents demonstrate their availability and interest in their children's lives, leading to deeper connections and better understanding. *The predictability of these interactions can help establish a routine that children can rely on, providing them with a stable foundation for expressing their thoughts and emotions.*

One critical advantage of establishing consistent communication spaces is the opportunity for parents to listen actively to their children. When children feel heard and understood, they are more likely to share their experiences openly. Regular conversations also allow parents to stay informed about their children's daily activities, challenges, and achievements. This knowledge strengthens the parent-child bond and enables parents to provide appropriate support and guidance.

Consistent communication spaces can enhance the parent-child relationship and improve children's emotional intelligence. Through regular conversations, children learn to articulate their feelings and thoughts, developing crucial communication skills that will benefit them throughout their lives. These rituals provide a safe space for children to express themselves without fear of judgment, fostering emotional growth and self-awareness.

Moreover, establishing talk rituals can help prevent misunderstandings and conflicts within the family. Parents can address issues proactively and resolve disputes before they escalate by creating a designated time for open dialogue. Regular communication promotes transparency and honesty, reducing the likelihood of miscommunication or pent-up emotions that can strain relationships.

Consistent communication spaces also serve as an opportunity for parents to model effective communication techniques. By engaging in respectful conversations with their children, parents demonstrate the importance of active listening, empathy, and constructive dialogue. These positive behaviors can influence how children communicate with others outside the family unit, shaping their interpersonal skills and relationships in the future.

Ultimately, the benefits of regular communication rituals extend beyond immediate family dynamics. By establishing a culture of open dialogue, parents lay the groundwork for healthy communication habits that can positively impact all areas of their children's lives, from school interactions to friendships and future relationships. Consistent communication spaces create a supportive environment where children feel valued, heard, and understood—a foundation for solid lifelong emotional bonds.

. . . .

ESTABLISHING A RELIABLE
Communication Framework

Establishing a structured framework that promotes consistent and meaningful communication within the family is essential for creating a reliable and predictable environment that encourages children to share their thoughts and feelings. This framework, tailored to each family's unique dynamics, fosters open dialogue, emotional safety, and trust. By incorporating specific components and guidelines, parents can cultivate an environment where children feel supported in expressing themselves authentically.

Selecting Optimal Time and Space

Choosing the right time and space for conversations is crucial in creating a conducive environment for communication. It is essential to select a setting where all family members feel comfortable, free from distractions, and able to engage fully in the discussion. Parents can signal the importance of these conversations by designating a specific time and place for these interactions and creating a sense of routine that children can rely on.

Formulating Guidelines for Respectful Communication

Establishing guidelines emphasizing respectful listening, openness, and non-judgmental communication is vital to fostering a safe space for sharing thoughts and feelings. Encouraging active listening without interruptions, offering empathy and understanding, and refraining from criticism or judgment can create an atmosphere where children feel validated and heard. Parents can ensure that conversations remain constructive and supportive by setting clear expectations for communication.

. . . .

INTEGRATING RITUALS into Daily Routines

Incorporating communication rituals into daily routines helps solidify the habit of regular interaction within the family. Whether it's a nightly chat before bedtime or a weekend walk in the park, integrating these rituals into daily life reinforces the importance of communication as a fundamental aspect of family dynamics. Consistency in these rituals builds trust and reliability, signaling children that their parents are available and attentive to their needs.

Utilizing Conversation Starters

Using prompts or conversation starters can facilitate dialogue during communication rituals, especially when starting discussions may feel challenging or awkward. Conversation starters can range from asking about highlights of the day to discussing emotions or thoughts on particular topics. These prompts help guide the conversation and encourage deeper engagement between parents and children.

Incorporating Feedback Mechanisms

Integrating feedback mechanisms allows both parent and child to provide input on the effectiveness of communication rituals. Parents can adapt and evolve these practices by soliciting feedback regularly to better suit their family's changing needs. Feedback mechanisms foster open communication about what works well and what may need adjustment, promoting continuous improvement in the quality of interactions.

In conclusion, by implementing this comprehensive framework centered around 'Talk Rituals,' parents can establish a reliable and predictable environment that encourages children to share their thoughts and feelings openly. The components of this model work together synergistically to create a space where communication flourishes, trust deepens, and relationships strengthen over time. Through consistent effort and commitment to this framework, families can build a solid foundation for healthy communication practices that endure various life challenges.

Establishing ***Talk Rituals*** is not just about adding another item to our busy schedules; it is about creating a foundational practice that nurtures our children's emotional and psychological well-being. We build a sturdy and reliable bridge to our children's inner worlds through the deliberate setting of time and space for regular conversations. This consistency is crucial because it lets children know they have a safe space to express themselves, which is vital for their development.

The benefits of these communication rituals are manifold. Not only do they foster a sense of security and belonging, but they also enhance our relationships with our children, making them feel valued and heard. The nightly chats or post-dinner walks become more than just routines; they transform into rich opportunities for connection and understanding. Through these moments, we demonstrate to our children that their thoughts and feelings matter and that we support and guide them.

Creating a predictable environment through these rituals reassures children that they can share their thoughts and feelings without fear of judgment or dismissal. This openness paves the way for honest and meaningful conversations that might not occur without such a nurturing atmosphere. In these moments, we truly get to know our children, learning not just about their day-to-day activities but also about their hopes, fears, and dreams.

As we explore the power of parent-child conversations in the remaining chapters, let us remember the profound impact of these simple yet effective rituals. They are not just methods of communication; they are lifelines that keep us connected to our children in a world that often moves too fast.

By integrating these practices into our daily lives, we enhance our current relationships and set the stage for a lifetime of open, honest, and loving communication. Let us cherish these moments of connection, for they are the threads that weave the tapestry of family life, filled with warmth, understanding, and mutual respect.

Chapter 8: Digging Deeper: The Power of Open-Ended Questions

Can Open-Ended Questions Truly Bridge the Gap?

In the soft glow of the evening, with the kitchen bathed in the warm light of a setting sun, Julia stood over her simmering pot of stew, stirring slowly. The scent of thyme and rosemary mingled with her thoughts, which wandered to her son, Michael, a quiet boy of nine who spoke little but thought deeply. Lately, she sensed a withdrawal in him, a retreat into a shell she couldn't penetrate with her usual barrage of "Did you have a good day?" and "Was your test okay?"

As she tasted the stew and added a pinch more salt, Julia's mind raced through conversations past, those filled with monosyllabic responses that frustrated her attempts to connect. She remembered an article about open-ended questions and their power to unlock more profound insights into a child's mind. The kitchen clock ticked audibly, marking time as she considered this new approach.

Later that evening at dinner, Julia tried anew under the soft hum of the dining room light. "Michael," she began tentatively as he poked at his carrots, "if you could invent something that would make you very happy, what would it be?" Her heart hung on his response; this was no ordinary question from their usual script.

Michael paused, his fork mid-air. His eyes brightened slightly—a subtle but noticeable shift. He laid his fork gently against the china and thought for a moment that seemed to stretch between them like the vast expanse of ocean. "A machine," he finally said slowly but surely, "that could read people's emotions so no one would be misunderstood."

The answer struck Julia as both profound and telling. She realized there were layers to her son that simple yes-no questions had never reached. That night, they talked more than they had in months—about school not just as a place but as a world of interactions and feelings.

Outside their window, leaves rustled in the gentle night breeze like quiet applause for this new opening chapter between mother and son. As Julia listened to Michael describe his world more vividly than ever before, using sketches from his imagination rather than direct answers from reality's surface-level inquiries, she wondered how many other secrets lay hidden beneath simple nods and one-word replies.

Could other parents find beneath their children's silence an ocean deep with thoughts waiting to be explored through a shift in questioning?

Unlock the Hidden Depths of Your Child's Mind

The art of conversation with a child is akin to tending a garden. It requires patience, nurturing, and the right tools to encourage growth. Open-ended questions are particularly potent among these tools, fostering an environment where children feel heard and valued. This chapter delves into why such questions are indispensable in pursuing meaningful parent-child dialogues.

Open-ended questions do more than solicit information; they invite the child to think and reflect, offering insights into their feelings and thoughts that might otherwise remain obscured. Unlike closed questions that corner responses into simple 'yes' or 'no' categories, open-ended inquiries encourage a narrative, a story—allowing a child to paint their world vividly. This enhances the depth of conversations and strengthens the bond between parent and child by building mutual trust and understanding.

. . . .

THE ART OF QUESTIONING

Learning the importance of using open-ended questions is the first step toward transforming your interactions. Each question you pose can be a stepping stone towards a deeper understanding of your child's mental and emotional landscape. By asking questions that require more than a one-word answer, you encourage your child to articulate their thoughts and emotions more fully.

Crafting Conversations

Practicing crafting these questions is not about following a strict script but rather understanding the essence of curiosity about another's experience. It involves a subtle balance between knowing when to probe further and when to listen. This chapter will provide practical strategies for parents to refine their questioning techniques, ensuring they are open-ended yet specific enough to guide children into deeper levels of thinking.

Emotional Insights Through Dialogue

One of the most profound benefits of mastering open-ended questions is the ability to gain insights into a child's emotions.

When children are given the space to express themselves without judgment, they reveal more than just surface-level information—they share their hopes, fears, and dreams. This chapter will explore how parents can become adept at interpreting these disclosures, using them to foster empathy and support in their parenting approach.

By integrating these practices into daily conversations, parents can unlock profound narratives at the heart of their child's inner world. These narratives are crucial; they form the foundation upon which children understand themselves and their place within the family and the wider world.

This exploration isn't merely academic—it's a journey towards emotional connectivity and resilience. Through thoughtful dialogue inspired by well-crafted open-ended questions, parents have an opportunity not only to guide but also to inspire their children toward greater self-awareness and emotional maturity.

By embracing this approach, we move beyond mere conversation and venture into a realm where each dialogue enriches the relationships we cherish most deeply. Thus, as we advance through this chapter, let us commit to mastering the art of asking to better know and nurture the young minds we are privileged to guide.

Open-ended questions are powerful tools for fostering meaningful conversations with your children; by asking questions that cannot be answered with a simple "yes" or "no," you encourage your child to express their thoughts and feelings more deeply. *These questions prompt reflection and introspection, opening the door to richer dialogue and a deeper understanding of your child's inner world.* When you ask open-ended questions, show your child that you value their perspective and are genuinely interested in what they say.

Unlike closed-ended questions that limit responses, open-ended inquiries invite exploration and elaboration. They encourage children to share their ideas, emotions, and experiences in a way that simple yes-no queries cannot. *This type of questioning can lead to more profound insights into your child's thoughts, beliefs, and concerns,* giving you a window into their unique worldview. Using open-ended questions regularly creates a safe space for your child to express themselves authentically.

Open-ended questions promote active listening and empathy, requiring you to truly engage with your child's responses. Instead of rushing to provide solutions or opinions, you can listen attentively and understand your child's perspective without judgment. *This practice strengthens the bond between parent and child,* fostering trust and emotional connection through meaningful conversations.

Asking open-ended questions also cultivates critical thinking skills in children, encouraging them to analyze situations, consider different viewpoints, and articulate their thoughts coherently. By challenging them to reflect on complex issues through thoughtful responses, you help develop their communication abilities and emotional intelligence. *These skills are invaluable for navigating relationships and understanding oneself,* making open-ended questioning essential for nurturing well-rounded individuals.

In the next section, explore the power of open-ended questions further as we delve into crafting inquiries that inspire deeper conversations with your child.

Crafting questions that encourage children to think and express more profoundly shifts the focus to creating a space for genuine exploration and understanding. *Open-ended questions* are pivotal in steering conversations toward richer insights and emotional depth. When formulating these questions, it is crucial to prioritize curiosity and empathy. By phrasing inquiries in a way that invites reflection and introspection, parents can foster an environment where children feel valued and understood.

The art of crafting open-ended questions is their ability to elicit thoughtful responses. Instead of seeking simple yes or no answers, these questions prompt children to delve into their thoughts, feelings, and experiences; by asking "why," "how," or "what do you think about...," parents can spark meaningful dialogues that unveil the intricacies of a child's inner world. This approach enhances communication and nurtures a sense of trust and openness between parent and child.

Encouraging children to think critically through open-ended questions fosters cognitive development. Children sharpen their analytical skills by engaging in conversations that require them to articulate their perspectives and learn to express themselves more clearly. This practice helps them develop a deeper understanding of their emotions and thoughts while honing their communication ability.

Crafting open-ended questions serves as a gateway to empathy. When parents pose inquiries that invite children to share their feelings and viewpoints without judgment, it cultivates a sense of validation and acceptance. This empathetic exchange reinforces the emotional bond between parent and child, fostering a supportive environment where authentic communication thrives.

Through open-ended questions, parents gain valuable insights into their child's unique worldview. By encouraging children to elaborate on their experiences and emotions, parents can better understand their perspectives and concerns. This deeper level of communication strengthens the parent-child relationship. It equips parents with the knowledge needed to provide appropriate support and guidance.

Practicing the art of crafting open-ended questions requires patience and attentiveness. It involves:

- Actively listening to children's responses.
- Asking follow-up questions that delve deeper into their thoughts.
- Creating a safe space for honest expression.

By honing these skills, parents can facilitate meaningful conversations that nurture mutual understanding and emotional connection.

Incorporating open-ended questions into daily interactions with children is a powerful tool for promoting self-reflection. By encouraging children to explore their beliefs, values, and emotions through conversation, parents empower them to develop self-awareness and reflective skills. This practice lays the foundation for healthy emotional growth and fosters a sense of autonomy and confidence in children.

In essence, crafting open-ended questions is not merely about stimulating dialogue but about fostering deep connections rooted in empathy, understanding, and mutual respect. Through thoughtful questioning, parents can unlock profound insights into their child's inner world, nurturing a relationship built on trust, communication, and emotional intimacy.

When engaging children in conversations using open-ended questions, it's essential to pay close attention to their responses.

Reactions to these inquiries can offer insights into a child's emotions and thoughts. Parents can uncover valuable information that may not have been shared otherwise by observing how they express themselves. *Children's responses to open-ended questions can provide a window into their inner world,* offering parents a deeper understanding of their feelings, concerns, and perspectives.

Listening attentively to a child's responses is crucial in gaining insights into their emotions and thoughts. *Parents* can pick up on subtle cues that reveal more about their inner state by actively focusing on what the child is saying. *Non-verbal cues* such as body language, facial expressions, and tone of voice can also offer valuable information about how the child feels. *Being present and engaged during these conversations* enables parents to connect more profoundly with their children and foster a sense of trust and openness.

Encouraging further elaboration on responses to open-ended questions can lead to deeper insights into a child's emotions and thoughts. *Asking follow-up questions that delve into specific aspects of their initial answers* can help uncover underlying motivations, fears, or desires that the child may not have articulated initially. *Prompting them to reflect* on their feelings and experiences through additional inquiries can stimulate introspection and self-awareness.

Respecting the child's perspective is paramount when seeking insights into their emotions and thoughts through open-ended inquiries. *Acknowledging their feelings without judgment or criticism* creates a safe space for them to express themselves honestly. **Validating their feelings** by showing empathy and understanding fosters a sense of emotional security and encourages open communication. *Parents respect their individuality by honoring the child's viewpoint* and strengthening the parent-child bond.

Recognizing patterns in a child's responses to open-ended questions can offer valuable insights into recurring themes or concerns in their lives. *Parents* can better understand their children's emotional development and thought processes by noting similarities or changes in their answers. *Identifying consistent themes in* their responses may indicate areas where the child requires additional support, guidance, or reassurance.

Creating a nurturing environment for open dialogue through open-ended questions is essential in gaining insights into a child's emotions and thoughts. *Establishing trust, empathy, and active listening as foundational elements* of parent-child conversations encourages children to share more openly and honestly. *Building a culture of communication-based* on mutual respect and understanding cultivates emotional intelligence and strengthens family relationships.

In conclusion, the power of open-ended questions lies in prompting children to elaborate on their thoughts and in providing parents with invaluable insights into their emotions and perspectives. By engaging in meaningful conversations with children using open-ended inquiries, parents can deepen their connection with their children, nurture emotional intelligence, and create a supportive environment for growth and self-expression.

The transformative power of open-ended questions marks a pivotal step in enhancing family communication. By encouraging children to think and articulate their feelings comprehensively, these inquiries deepen mutual understanding and fortify emotional connections.

Step 1: Understanding the Importance of Open-Ended Questions
Open-ended questions are essential as they compel a child to engage more fully with the conversation. These questions demand more than a simple 'yes' or 'no'; they require thoughtful, often introspective responses. This kind of questioning nurtures an environment where children feel valued and understood, fostering their ability to express complex thoughts and emotions.

Step 2: Crafting Open-Ended Questions
Begin by identifying the topics you wish to explore with your child. Develop a list of questions inviting expansive answers that encourage your child to describe, explain, or reflect. It's crucial to frame these questions unbiasedly to ensure the child's responses are entirely their own. Use prompts like "What do you think about...?" or "How did that experience feel for you?" to open up the dialogue.

Step 3: Gaining Insights Through Open-Ended Inquiries
Once the child begins to respond, active listening is key. Pay close attention, not just to the words but also to the emotions underlying them. Reflect on their answers and use this deeper understanding to further inquire about their thoughts and feelings. This iterative process of asking and listening helps clarify and expand the conversation, providing richer insights into your child's inner world.

Implementing this approach effectively requires patience and practice. It might initially feel more laborious than asking straightforward questions. Still, the depth of understanding gained is well worth the effort. Each step should be seen as an opportunity to strengthen the bond with your child, turning everyday conversations into moments of genuine connection and insight.

• • • •

BY MASTERING THESE steps, you equip yourself with a powerful tool beyond mere communication, reaching into the heart of thoughtful and empathetic engagement with your child's world. This practice enhances your relationship and empowers your child, giving them the voice they need to express their most intricate thoughts and feelings. Through this ongoing dialogue, you lay a foundation of trust and understanding that supports their growth into thoughtful, articulate individuals.

Chapter 9: Emotional Intelligence in Action: Coaching Kids on Self-Expression

Can Emotional Coaching Mend a Fractured Relationship?

Thomas walked down the narrow, sunlit path that led through the park, his thoughts as scattered as the autumn leaves crunched under his feet. His daughter, Emily, had been distant lately—her once vibrant demeanor dimmed to a sullen silence that hung heavily between them. Thomas remembered how they laughed here, her small hand gripping his as they chased fleeting butterflies.

The chill in the air mirrored the growing chill in their relationship. Thomas watched a young father hoist his giggling child onto his shoulders, and he longed for those simpler times. He wondered if emotional coaching could bridge the gap between him and Emily.

Could helping her articulate her feelings restore the warmth they once shared?

As he sat on a worn wooden bench overlooking a pond where ducks glided effortlessly across the water, Thomas recalled reading about emotional intelligence. It was about understanding one's emotions and effectively communicating them—skills he wished he'd learned earlier in life. Perhaps teaching Emily these skills could open new avenues for connection.

A rustle of leaves drew his attention to a squirrel scurrying up an oak tree, its slight body tense with alertness. Thomas related to that tension; it mirrored his feelings of unease about broaching emotional topics with Emily. How does one even begin to teach emotional literacy? He worried about saying the wrong thing, pushing her further away.

He rose from the bench and continued walking, resolving to try despite his fears. After all, wasn't it part of loving someone showing up for them in ways that mattered? The path curved ahead, obscured slightly by overhanging branches that whispered in the gentle breeze.

Could finding the right words be the key to unlocking his daughter's heart again?

Unlocking Emotional Wisdom: A Blueprint for Parent-Child Connection

Emotional intelligence is more than a buzzword; it's a pivotal skill set that influences our children's ability to navigate their feelings, relationships, and challenges. At the heart of emotional intelligence lies the practice of ***emotional coaching***, a powerful parenting tool that fosters self-awareness and resilience in children. This chapter delves into how parents can guide their children in recognizing, articulating, and managing their emotions effectively. The goal? To arm the next generation with the tools they need for emotional clarity and maturity.

Emotional coaching helps bridge the gap between feeling and expressing. Parents teaching kids to label their emotions accurately lays the groundwork for vibrant emotional health and communication skills. This process enhances a child's capacity to engage with others empathetically, an essential component of developing meaningful relationships and social networks.

The Foundation of Emotional Coaching

The role of emotional coaching extends beyond correcting behavior; it involves understanding the *why* behind feelings. When children face emotional upheavals or conflicts, a parent's response can either open a dialogue or shut it down. This chapter outlines how parents can use moments of emotional intensity as opportunities for teaching and connection rather than occasions for discipline or dismissal.

Articulation Leads to Empowerment

One cannot underestimate the power of naming an emotion. Learning to verbalize feelings is akin to finding a map in a dense forest for a child. It provides direction and clarity, reducing anxiety and confusion. We will explore techniques parents can use to help their children articulate complex emotions, thus equipping them with better control over their reactions and decisions.

Conversational Pathways to Emotional Maturity

Guided conversation practices are invaluable tools in this educational journey. They assist children in navigating their emotional landscapes and teach them how to express these landscapes clearly and respectfully to others. Such practices strengthen the child's voice, ensuring they are heard, understood, and valued.

Through these conversations, children learn more about themselves and their relational environments. They begin to see how their words impact others, fostering a sense of responsibility and empathy. Moreover, these discussions can become foundational pillars in building trust between parent and child, transforming potential conflicts into bonding and mutual understanding moments.

The Ripple Effects of Emotional Literacy

The benefits of nurturing emotional literacy extend far beyond childhood. Adolescents with high emotional intelligence are better equipped to handle the pressures of school life, from academic responsibilities to social dynamics. As adults, they continue reaping the benefits through healthier relationships and more effective communication skills in both personal and professional contexts.

By prioritizing emotional coaching in daily interactions with our children, we do more than help them manage immediate feelings—we set them on a path toward long-term emotional wellbeing and success. This chapter provides parents with practical strategies designed to address current emotions and foster an enduring emotional strength that will serve their children for a lifetime.

In exploring emotional intelligence through parental coaching, we aim to transform everyday interactions into profound learning experiences that significantly impact our children's future happiness and achievements.

Understanding the role of emotional coaching in a child's emotional development is crucial for fostering healthy self-expression. Emotional coaching involves guiding children to recognize, understand, and manage their emotions effectively. By providing support and guidance in navigating their feelings, parents can help children develop emotional intelligence, which is essential for building strong interpersonal relationships. Emotional coaching empowers children to communicate their emotions constructively and express themselves authentically.

Emotional coaching is a foundation for teaching children how to navigate the complex landscape of emotions. It allows parents to connect with their children deeper, creating a safe space for open dialogue about feelings. By validating children's emotions and helping them understand what they are experiencing, parents can build trust and strengthen their bond with their children. *This process lays the groundwork for developing empathy and self-awareness.*

Children who receive emotional coaching are better equipped to regulate their emotions. They learn how to identify different feelings, understand the triggers behind them, and develop coping strategies to manage intense emotions. This skill set is invaluable in helping children navigate challenging situations and conflicts with resilience and maturity. *Emotional coaching empowers children to respond thoughtfully rather than react impulsively.*

Through emotional coaching, parents can help children cultivate practical communication skills. By teaching children how to articulate their emotions clearly and express themselves assertively yet respectfully, parents equip them with the tools needed for healthy social interactions. *This practice fosters self-confidence and encourages children to advocate for their needs while considering the feelings of others.*

Continues...

Teaching children to identify, articulate, and manage their emotions effectively is crucial to nurturing their emotional intelligence. By guiding children in understanding their feelings and expressing them clearly, we equip them with essential life skills that will benefit them in various aspects of their development.

Empowering children to recognize and communicate their emotions fosters self-awareness. It lays the foundation for healthier relationships as they grow.

Encouraging children to label their emotions is the first step in helping them develop emotional intelligence. Teaching them the vocabulary to express their feelings enables them to navigate their emotional landscape more effectively. This practice enhances their ability to understand themselves and allows them to communicate their needs and concerns to others more clearly.

Through active listening and validation, we can create a safe space for children to share their emotions without fear of judgment. Validating a child's feelings by acknowledging and accepting them helps build trust and fosters open communication. *By showing empathy and understanding*, we teach children that their emotions are valid and worthy of attention, instilling a sense of self-worth and emotional security.

Guiding children in managing their emotions involves teaching them coping strategies to deal with complicated feelings constructively. By offering tools such as deep breathing exercises, journaling, or talking about their emotions, we help children develop healthy ways to regulate their feelings. *Encouraging mindfulness practices* can also aid children in becoming more attuned to their emotions and better equipped to respond thoughtfully rather than impulsively.

Modeling healthy emotional expression is vital in teaching children how to manage their feelings effectively. Children learn by observing adults' behavior, so parents and caregivers must demonstrate positive ways of expressing and dealing with emotions. ***By being open about our feelings*** and demonstrating healthy coping mechanisms, we provide children with valuable examples to emulate.

Creating a supportive environment where children feel comfortable sharing emotions is vital for fostering emotional intelligence. By prioritizing open communication, active listening, and empathy, we can cultivate a space where children feel heard, understood, and valued. ***Encouraging a culture of emotional openness*** strengthens parent-child bonds and equips children with the tools they need to navigate the complexities of their inner world.

In essence, teaching children to identify, articulate, and manage their emotions effectively is an ongoing process that requires patience, empathy, and consistency. By instilling in children the skills to understand and express their feelings authentically, we empower them to navigate life's challenges with resilience and emotional maturity. ***Investing time and effort in nurturing a child's emotional intelligence is an invaluable gift that will benefit them throughout their lives.***

Emotional Intelligence Framework: Navigating Parent-Child Conversations

The framework presented here is a structured approach to nurturing emotional intelligence through parent-child interactions. It guides parents to navigate the complexities of emotions and communication with their children, promoting healthy emotional expression and regulation. Let's delve into each model component to understand how it can be applied in real-life situations.

Recognizing Emotional Moments

The first step in the framework is to recognize emotional moments as opportunities for intimacy and teaching. ***This involves being*** *attentive to subtle cues from your child* that indicate they are experiencing strong emotions. *Acknowledging these moments creates a space for open dialogue and connection*, setting the stage for meaningful conversations about feelings.

Listening Empathetically

Listening empathetically to your child's emotional expressions without dismissal or judgment is crucial for fostering trust and understanding. *This component emphasizes active listening*, where you focus on your child's words, tone, and body language to grasp the full extent of their emotions. *Empathy builds a foundation of support and validation* that encourages children to express themselves freely.

Labeling Emotions

Labeling emotions simply and understandably helps children identify and articulate their feelings accurately. *By giving names to emotions, you empower your child with vocabulary* to express themselves effectively. *This clarity aids in self-awareness and communication*, fostering emotional intelligence and resilience.

Validating Feelings

Validating your child's feelings by acknowledging their emotional experience as real and significant is essential for building trust and confidence. *When you validate emotions, you show empathy* and create a safe space for your child to share their inner world without fear of judgment. *This validation strengthens the parent-child bond* and promotes emotional wellbeing.

Offering Guidance

Offering guidance on problem-solving while respecting your child's ability to cope demonstrates trust in their capacity to manage emotions. *Guidance should be supportive rather than prescriptive*, encouraging autonomy and self-reliance in handling challenges. *Empowering children with problem-solving skills* enhances their emotional competence.

Co-Creating Strategies

Co-creating emotional regulation and expression strategies empowers children to navigate their emotions effectively.

Involving your child in developing coping mechanisms instills a sense of ownership over their emotional wellbeing. *This collaborative approach fosters independence* and equips children with lifelong emotional management skills.

In summary, this framework emphasizes the importance of emotional coaching in parent-child conversations, guiding parents through a supportive process that nurtures emotional intelligence in children. By recognizing, listening, labeling, validating, guiding, and co-creating strategies with children, parents can cultivate an environment that promotes expressive clarity, emotional maturity, and resilience in their young ones.

Emotional coaching is pivotal in nurturing a child's ability to express themselves effectively and healthily. By guiding our children through identifying, articulating, and managing their emotions, we equip them with invaluable tools that extend far beyond childhood. This chapter has explored the how and **why** of emotional coaching—emphasizing its irreplaceable role in emotional development and interpersonal relationships.

The journey begins with helping children recognize their own emotions. Imagine the profound impact of a child learning to say, "I feel sad," rather than acting out. This simple act of self-expression opens doors to deeper understanding and support.

Through such clarity, children learn to navigate their internal landscapes, and this emotional mapping is critical as they grow.

Furthermore, our discussions around articulating emotions take this understanding a step further. It's one thing to recognize an emotion; it's another to express it constructively. When children learn to communicate their feelings effectively, they engage more positively with peers and adults. This skill is foundational for building lasting, healthy relationships throughout their lives.

Finally, the guided conversation practices we've introduced serve as the practical application of these concepts. They are not just exercises but essential, everyday tools that enhance emotional literacy. Through these conversations, children gain confidence in their emotional expression, fostering resilience and a strong sense of self.

We do more than teach skills by embedding these practices into our daily interactions. We demonstrate empathy, validate experiences, and constructively model how to manage emotions. This approach does not simplify the complex emotions everyone navigates; instead, it acknowledges and respects them, offering a path toward emotional maturity.

Let us continue to understand that our role in emotional coaching is not just about correcting or directing but about empowering our children to understand and express their feelings. The skills they develop will help them in their current interactions and form the basis of their future emotional wellbeing.

In embracing these practices, we create an environment where emotional expression is heard and valued—a gift our children will carry with them, shaping their world and the world of others as they grow.

Chapter 10: The Echo of Assurance: Building Confidence in Communication

Can Consistent Reassurance Truly Mold a Child's Confidence in Communication?

The sun was setting, casting long shadows across the playground where Michael watched his son, Tommy, hesitate at the edge of a group of chattering children. The cool breeze carried the distant laughter and occasional shout to where he stood, hands buried deep in his jacket pockets, eyes tracing his son's every move.

Tommy moved forward a step, then stopped, his gaze fixed on the ground. Michael felt a familiar tightness in his chest—the silent echo of Tommy's struggles with communication. Just last week, they had celebrated a small victory when Tommy had asked a neighbor's child to pass him the ball. Today, however, the reluctance was back like an unwelcome visitor.

Michael remembered his father's stern warnings not to show fear or hesitation. He shook off the memory as if dislodging snow from his shoulders. He knew better now; reassurance and positive reinforcement were tools he chose to wield in shaping his son's confidence.

A little girl broke away from the group and approached Tommy. She said something that made him look up, and for a moment, there was a flicker of engagement in his eyes before it vanished like smoke into thin air. Michael watched as Tommy nodded slowly but didn't move towards the group.

The crunch of gravel underfoot brought him back from his reverie as another parent passed by with a nod. Michael returned it mechanically, his mind weaving through past conversations with child psychologists and endless articles about child development he had read late into many nights. They all echoed the importance of acknowledging Tommy's small effort toward communication.

Was it enough? Could these moments of gentle encouragement truly build a fortress strong enough to house his son's burgeoning confidence?

He walked over to Tommy, knelt beside him with a smile that felt like sunshine after rain, and whispered, "That looked tough, but you did well listening to her." The simplicity of recognizing effort over success seemed counterintuitive yet profound.

As they walked home together under the canopy of an indigo sky pierced by early stars, Michael pondered how each small acknowledgment might pave stones on Tommy's path to self-assurance in communication.

Could these consistent reassurances really be the threads weaving stronger connections between them?

Unleashing Confidence: The Power of Reassurance in Parent-Child Conversations

In the intricate dance of parent-child communication, the steps to foster confidence through consistent reassurance can profoundly influence the rhythm of lifelong relationships. As we delve deeper into the nuances of effective communication within families, it becomes evident that the echoes of our words resonate far beyond the immediate conversation. ***Consistent reassurance*** enhances a child's ability to communicate and fortifies their self-esteem and trust in their voice. This chapter explores how positive reinforcement after successful exchanges can establish a robust foundation for open and honest dialogue, ultimately shaping a child's communicative competence and confidence.

Understanding the pivotal role of ***reassurance is*** a cornerstone in cultivating an environment where children feel valued and understood.

By acknowledging and celebrating their efforts in communication, we reinforce the behaviors that contribute to practical discourse. This practice boosts a child's confidence and encourages them to engage more willingly and constructively in future conversations. Here, we will dissect how such reinforcement can be implemented effectively to nurture a supportive dialogue between parent and child.

The essence of positive reinforcement lies in its ability to transform ordinary conversations into extraordinary lessons in trust and mutual respect. Each positive interaction serves as a building block for a resilient relationship that can withstand the challenges of growth and change. We will explore various techniques parents can employ to ensure that their affirmation is both meaningful and impactful, thereby enhancing the family's communication quality.

Moreover, this chapter emphasizes the importance of creating a *cycle of confidence* through continuous encouragement and support. As parents consistently apply these principles, they not only foster a secure environment for their children to express themselves but also lay the groundwork for developing critical life skills in communication. The insights provided here aim to equip parents with practical strategies that can be seamlessly integrated into daily interactions, thereby transforming potential misunderstandings into opportunities for growth and connection.

As we approach the culmination of our exploration into parent-child conversations, it is crucial to reflect on how these communication practices integrate with broader family dynamics.

The strategies discussed throughout this book are designed to address isolated incidents of miscommunication and build enduring bonds that support both parent and child throughout various stages of life. By mastering these communication techniques, families can look forward to a future where every member feels heard, understood, and valued.

By engaging with these concepts, readers are invited on a transformative journey that promises improved communication skills and a deeper understanding of their children's needs and perspectives. This journey fosters an empathetic approach to parenting that recognizes heartfelt conversations' profound impact on a child's development and wellbeing.

This exploration is not merely about avoiding conflict but embracing opportunities for connection that foster long-term resilience and happiness within the family unit. Through this chapter's guidance, parents will be well-equipped to lead conversations that resolve misunderstandings and strengthen the fabric of family life through trust, empathy, and unconditional support.

Consistent reassurance plays a crucial role in boosting a child's communicative efforts. When children feel supported and encouraged in their communication attempts, they are more likely to engage openly and confidently in conversations. Parents who provide positive reinforcement after successful communication exchanges help reinforce these behaviors, leading to a cycle of increased confidence and trust in communication. Acknowledging and praising a child's efforts in expressing themselves fosters a sense of security and validation, encouraging them to share their thoughts and feelings more freely.

Reassurance is vital in nurturing a child's communication skills. By consistently showing understanding and appreciation for their attempts at expressing themselves, parents create a safe space for their children to communicate without fear of judgment or criticism. This positive environment allows children to explore their thoughts and emotions, leading to more meaningful interactions with their parents.

Children thrive on positive feedback. When parents recognize and celebrate their children's communicative successes, it boosts their confidence and motivates them to continue engaging in conversations. This encouragement creates a sense of accomplishment and reinforces the importance of effective communication, setting the stage for more open and honest dialogues between parent and child.

Consistency is essential when it comes to reassurance. By regularly acknowledging and affirming a child's communicative efforts, parents help build a strong foundation of trust and confidence in communication. This ongoing support empowers children to express themselves authentically and strengthens the parent-child bond through meaningful interactions.

Embrace the power of consistent reassurance to elevate your child's communication skills.

Parents can create an environment where open, honest dialogues flourish by recognizing the value of consistent reassurance in boosting a child's communicative efforts. Through positive reinforcement and continuous encouragement, children develop the confidence to express themselves effectively, fostering deeper connections with their parents. The echo of assurance resonates through each conversation, building a foundation of trust and understanding that enriches the parent-child relationship.

Positive reinforcement is a powerful tool in shaping a child's behavior and boosting their confidence in communication. Parents can encourage their children to engage more actively and confidently in conversations by implementing positive reinforcement techniques after successful communication exchanges. *Acknowledging and praising a child's efforts* to express themselves effectively can go a long way in reinforcing those behaviors. When children feel validated and appreciated for their communicative efforts, they are likelier to continue engaging in positive communication patterns.

Celebrating small victories in communication can significantly impact a child's self-esteem and willingness to communicate openly. When parents highlight moments of successful communication, it reinforces the idea that their children are capable of expressing themselves effectively. This positive feedback loop can increase the child's confidence and sense of achievement.

Encouragement and praise after successful conversations create a supportive environment where children feel valued and understood.

Using specific praise can be particularly effective in reinforcing positive communication behaviors. Instead of general statements like "good job," parents can provide more targeted and meaningful feedback. For example, saying, "I appreciate how you explained your feelings clearly," or "You did a great job listening attentively," helps children understand precisely what they did well in the conversation. *Specific praise* reinforces positive behaviors and helps children identify their strengths in communication.

Incorporating rewards as part of positive reinforcement can further motivate children to engage actively in conversations. Simple rewards such as extra playtime, choosing an activity, or small treats can incentivize children to participate enthusiastically in communication exchanges. By associating positive experiences with effective communication, children are more likely to view conversations as enjoyable and rewarding.

Consistency is vital when using positive reinforcement techniques. Regularly acknowledging and praising a child's communicative efforts helps establish a pattern of encouragement and support. Children who receive consistent positive feedback for their communication skills are more likely to feel confident and secure in expressing themselves. *Reinforcing positive behaviors consistently* reinforces the idea that effective communication is valued and appreciated within the family dynamic.

By implementing positive reinforcement techniques after successful communication exchanges, parents can play a crucial role in building their children's confidence in expressing themselves. *Celebrating small victories*, using specific praise, incorporating rewards, and consistently reinforcing positive behaviors create a supportive environment where children feel empowered to communicate openly and authentically. Through these practices, parents can foster a sense of accomplishment and self-assurance in their children's communicative abilities, laying the foundation for intense, trusting relationships built on open dialogue and understanding.

Consistent encouragement and support form the bedrock of building confidence and trust in communication between parents and children. By continuously acknowledging and reinforcing positive communication behaviors, parents can create a cycle of assurance that strengthens the child's willingness to engage openly.

After successful conversations, encouragement is a powerful motivator, instilling a sense of accomplishment and validation in the child. This positive reinforcement boosts the child's self-esteem and nurtures a sense of security in expressing their thoughts and emotions.

Continuous encouragement fosters a safe space for children to communicate, knowing that their efforts will be met with appreciation and acknowledgment. When parents consistently praise their children for effective communication, it conveys that their words are valued and respected. This validation reinforces the child's belief in their ability to authenticate themselves, leading to more meaningful conversations and deeper connections within the family unit.

By cultivating a cycle of confidence through ongoing support, parents can create an environment where children feel empowered to share their thoughts without fear of judgment. This sense of security allows for open, honest dialogues that strengthen the bond between parent and child. Through consistent encouragement, parents can instill in their children a sense of self-assurance that extends beyond communication skills, benefiting them in various aspects of life.

Continuous communication support reinforces the idea that mistakes are part of learning and growth, encouraging children to take risks in expressing themselves without the fear of failure. When parents provide unwavering encouragement, it builds resilience in children, teaching them to navigate challenges with confidence and perseverance. This nurturing environment enhances communication skills and equips children with essential life skills that will serve them well into adulthood.

Building trust through continuous encouragement lays the foundation for healthy relationships based on open communication. Children who feel supported and validated in expressing themselves are more likely to seek guidance from their parents when faced with difficult situations. This trust allows for meaningful conversations where both parties feel heard and understood, fostering mutual respect and empathy within the family dynamic.

In conclusion, cultivating a cycle of confidence and trust in communication through continuous encouragement and support is essential for nurturing solid parent-child relationships. By consistently reinforcing positive communication behaviors, parents can empower their children to communicate effectively, build resilience, and foster deep connections based on trust and understanding. Through this ongoing practice, families can create a harmonious environment where every conversation becomes an opportunity for growth and connection.

Throughout this chapter, we have explored the profound impact of consistent reassurance and positive reinforcement on a child's ability to communicate confidently. By acknowledging and celebrating each successful exchange, parents can significantly enhance their child's willingness and ability to engage in open and meaningful conversations. This practice bolsters the child's confidence and deepens the trust between parent and child, creating a nurturing cycle of growth and understanding.

The essence of our discussion highlights the importance of ***continuous encouragement.*** As parents, the steady stream of support you provide after each communication attempt does more than acknowledge your child's efforts; it propels them to become more articulate and emotionally aware. This approach is crucial in helping children feel valued and understood within the family dynamic, which, in turn, fosters an environment where they can express themselves without fear of judgment or dismissal.

Moreover, the strategies discussed here are not isolated techniques but part of a broader, holistic approach to family communication.

They are vital tools that contribute to a supportive dialogue where every family member can thrive. By implementing these practices, parents can expect to see improvement not only in their children's communicative abilities but also in the overall emotional health of the family.

This chapter and the entire book serve as a guide to transforming everyday conversations into opportunities for bonding and mutual understanding. The principles we've outlined are designed to equip parents with the skills to navigate various stages of their child's development effectively. From tackling sensitive topics to celebrating small victories, each chapter builds on the last, culminating in a comprehensive blueprint for fostering lasting familial bonds.

As we conclude, remember that the journey of enhancing communication within your family is ongoing and ever-evolving. It requires patience, empathy, and, most importantly, a commitment to practicing the techniques discussed. By engaging with your child in ways that respect their feelings and encourage their thoughts, you set the foundation for a lifelong relationship where both parent and child feel genuinely heard and deeply connected.

Embrace these moments of conversation as precious opportunities to teach and learn from your child, strengthening the ties that bind your family together. In doing so, you are building better communicators and nurturing resilient individuals who can face the world with confidence and clarity.

Crafting Conversations That Last a Lifetime

As we draw to a close on our journey through the art of parent-child conversations, we must reflect on the profound impact our words and approaches can have on our relationships. The power of communication, as explored in these pages, is not just about talking more but about connecting deeper.

In applying the insights from this book, envision transforming daily interactions into opportunities for growth and bonding. Whether navigating a problematic topic or sharing a light-hearted moment, every conversation is a stepping stone towards a stronger relationship. Think of your new skills as tools in a kit, ready to build a bridge between hearts and minds.

We've covered strategies ranging from active listening to adjusting communication styles according to your child's developmental stage. These are not just theories but practical tools designed for real-world application. Implementing these techniques can turn misunderstandings into moments of mutual understanding and conflict into cooperation.

From Insight to Action

To truly benefit from this book, take these strategies beyond the pages. Start small: initiate a 'weekly check-in' with your child, using open-ended questions to explore their thoughts and feelings. Or, implement 'listening sessions' where the focus is entirely on understanding their perspective without immediately jumping to solutions.

Remember, the goal is not perfection but progress. Each conversation is an opportunity to practice and refine your skills. Over time, what may feel awkward or forced will become more natural and effective.

Embracing Limitations and Looking Forward

While this book provides a robust foundation for enhancing family communication, it's essential to acknowledge its limitations. Every child is unique, and specific suggestions may need adaptation. Furthermore, as society evolves, new challenges in parent-child communication will emerge, necessitating continuous learning and adaptation.

Future exploration could delve deeper into digital communication's role in family dynamics or how cultural differences influence family conversations. I encourage you to keep exploring and adapting the strategies discussed as you grow alongside your children.

A Call to Heartfelt Dialogue

Now is the time to take these insights from theory to practice. Let the ideas nourish your conversations. Embrace mistakes as part of the learning process and celebrate small victories in understanding each other better.

Let us not underestimate the power of heartfelt dialogue in creating lasting bonds that not only survive but thrive through life's challenges.

In Closing

As you continue to build stronger connections with your children through effective communication, remember that each word spoken in sincerity and love lays another brick in the foundation of a lifelong bond.

"Listen earnestly to anything your children want to tell you, no matter what. If you don't listen eagerly to the little stuff when they are

little, they won't tell you the big stuff when they are big because, to them, all of it has always been big stuff."

— Catherine M. Wallace

Don't miss out!

Visit the website below and you can sign up to receive emails whenever Perry L. Davidson publishes a new book. There's no charge and no obligation.

https://books2read.com/r/B-A-UIWNB-EXXZE

Did you love *Speaking Hearts: Unlocking the Power of Parent-Child Conversations*? Then you should read *Fandom Unveiled: Harnessing the Heartbeat of Sports Loyalties*[1] by Perry L. Davidson!

[2]

Thank you for choosing to embark on this journey through the pages of this exploration. You have taken a step towards not just understanding the phenomena of sports loyalties but also towards appreciating the profound impact it can have on identity and social connections.

This book is tailored specifically for anyone who finds themselves puzzled by their sudden emotional investment in a team or those curious about how sports influence social interactions and personal identity. Whether you are a new fan seeking to deepen your appreciation or a casual observer striving to understand your surroundings better, there is something in these pages for you.

---

1. https://books2read.com/u/3kNKrn

2. https://books2read.com/u/3kNKrn

As we turn these pages together, I invite you to dive deep into the stories and studies that explain why sports can mean so much. Let's explore how fandom molds identities, shapes communities, and even alters our emotional landscapes. By the end of this narrative, you will not only gain insight into what drives millions into the arms of sports teams but also appreciate how these allegiances enrich our lives.

Also by Perry L. Davidson

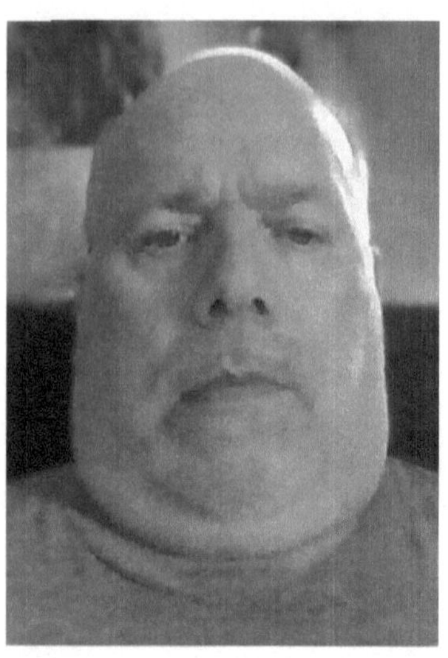

About the Author

At age 67, Perry L. Davidson is embarking on a journey that intertwines the culmination of a lifetime's experiences with fulfilling a long-held dream: publishing his first book. As a Navy veteran and a retired dispatcher, Perry L. Davidson brings a wealth of life experiences to his writing, which is marked by years of service, dedication, and a deep understanding of the human spirit.

Born and raised in Charleston, South Carolina, Perry L. Davidson spent his early years absorbing the stories and landscapes that would later become the backdrop for his narratives. His time in the Navy not only instilled in him a sense of discipline and resilience but also exposed him to a diversity of people and places, enriching his perspective and deepening his appreciation for the myriad ways in which life unfolds.

After his service, Perry L. Davidson transitioned to a career as a dispatcher. This role sharpened his ability to listen, empathize, and communicate effectively under pressure. These years were not just about managing crises but about understanding the stories behind each call. This experience honed his storytelling skills and fueled his passion for writing.

Now, in retirement, Perry L. Davidson has turned to the pen (or keyboard) as his tool for exploration and expression. His writing is a testament to his belief in the power of stories to connect, heal, and inspire. The themes of courage, perseverance, and the search for meaning that run through his work reflect his own life's journey.

Publishing his first book is a personal achievement for Perry L. Davidson and a gift to his readers. It offers insights and inspirations drawn from a well-lived life. As he steps into literature, he hopes to encourage others, regardless of age, to pursue their dreams and tell their stories, proving that it's always possible to start a new chapter.